OPTIONS TRADING

– LONG AND SHORT OPTIONS –

Sergey K. Aityan

Lincoln University, Oakland, California

Copyright © 2020 Sergey K. Aityan
All rights reserved.
Amazon KDP
ISBN: 979-8657512656
ASIN: B08BW5Y4TS

Preface

Trading options is an exciting and quite lucrative way of investing in the stock market. Options offer high leverage and protect from the excessive losses. On the other hand, options expose investors to the higher level of risk, surely making options trading not suitable for early beginners. You may be confused with the two statements made above about options protecting from the excessive losses and at the same time, exposing to the higher risk. Do not judge on the spot and learn options first. Options see many different types of risk.

Many books have been published about options trading and it looks like there is no need for one more book. However, books may be different, meeting specific needs of the readers. The purpose of this book is to provide the detailed fundamentals of options trading. This book discusses the nature of options, who makes options, how they are originated, traded, exercised, and assigned, what is the difference between long and short options, and what are the differences in trading strategies, goals, and the respective market conditions for using long and short options. The scope of this book is limited to single options, long and short. Which are described in a greater detail. This is the fundamental distinction of this book from many other similar books.

This book is in part an exert from a broader book on the stock market entitled "Stock Market Course, Part 1: Exchanges, Stocks, and Options" but contains additional important information targeting those, who want to learn the detailed fundamentals of options before investing.

More complex option opportunities come with the combination of options with stocks and options, such as covered and protective calls and puts, straddles, strangles, spreads butterflies, condors and other. A variety of such combinations including their usage, opportunities, as well as their pros and cons will be discussed in the separate book.

Sergey K. Aityan, PhD, DSc, Professor

Disclaimer: This book is presented solely for educational and entertainment purposes. The author and publisher are not offering it as investment, financial, legal, accounting, or other professional advice. This book contains general information regarding finance, investment, and legal aspects that is based on the author's own knowledge and experiences. It is published for general reference and is not intended to be a substitute for the advice of an investment or financial professional, accountant, or legal adviser. The publisher and the author disclaim any personal liability, either directly or indirectly, for the information or examples contained herein. Although the author and the publisher have made every effort to ensure the accuracy and completeness of the information presented here, they assume no responsibility for errors, inaccuracies, omissions, and inconsistencies. You should seek the services of a competent professional before beginning any investment activity.

Table of Contents (Brief)

1 Equities and Derivatives 1
2 The Notion of Options 5
3 Intrinsic and Extrinsic Values of Options 13
4 Options Trading 25
5 Option Leverage and Greeks 41
6 Long Options 51
7 Short Options 61
8 Naked Calls 67
9 Naked Puts 79
10 Trading Strategies with Single Options 89
11 Trend Strategies 109

Table of Contents (Detailed)

1 **Equities and Derivatives** 1
   1.1 Equities and Derivatives 1
   1.2 Investing in the Stocks Market is Hard Work 2
   1.3 Clearly Understand Your Investment Goal,
         Financial Capabilities, and Responsibilities 2
   Self-Testing Questions 3

2 **The Notion of Options** 5
   2.1 Options Basics 5
   2.2 The Rational for Using Options 7
   2.3 History of Options 8
        2.3.1 Thales of Miletus and Olive Presses 8
        2.3.2 Options in the Stock Market 9
   2.4 Listed Options in the Stock Market 9
   Self-Testing Questions 12

3 **Intrinsic and Extrinsic Values of Options** 13
   3.1 Two Components of Options Value 13
   3.2 Intrinsic Value of Options 14
   3.3 Extrinsic or Time Value of Options 16
   Self-Testing Questions and Exercises 24
        Questions 24
        Exercises 24

4 **Options Trading** 25
   4.1 The Size of Stock Options Market 25
   4.2 Option Contracts and Quotation 25
   4.3 Who Makes Options 28
   4.4 Trading Actions 29
   4.5 Dimensions of Option Trading Orders 31
   4.6 Option Exercise and Assignment 32
   4.7 Volume and Open Interest 34
   Self-Testing Questions and Exercises 38
        Questions 38
        Exercises 38

5 **Option Leverage and Greeks** 41
   5.1 Leverage Power of Options 41
   5.2 Option Exercise vs. Option Trading 42
   5.3 Option Greeks 42
        5.3.1 Historical vs. Implied Volatility 43

	5.3.2	Delta	44
	5.3.3	Gamma	45
	5.3.4	Vega	46
	5.3.5	Theta	46
	5.3.6	Rho	47
	5.3.7	Combination of Greeks	48
	5.3.8	Summary of Greeks	48
5.4	Options Offer Great Opportunities but be Careful with Them		49
Self-Testing Questions and Exercises			49
	Questions		49
	Exercises		49

6 Long Options 51

6.1	Operations and Hedging with Options	51
6.2	Long Calls and Puts	53
6.3	Closing Long Calls and Puts by Selling Them	54
6.4	Exercising Long Calls or Puts	55
6.5	Strategy with Long Options	58
Self-Testing Questions and Exercises		59
	Questions	59
	Exercises	59

7 Short Options 61

7.1	The Sense of Short Options	61
Self-Testing Questions and Exercises		65
	Questions	65
	Exercises	65

8 Naked Calls 67

8.1	Naked (Short) Calls	67
8.2	Gain/Loss with a Naked Call	74
8.3	Strategies with Naked Calls	76
Self-Testing Questions and Exercises		77
	Questions	77
	Exercises	77

9 Naked Puts 79

9.1	Naked (Short) Puts	79
9.2	Gain/Loss with a Naked Put	84
9.3	Strategies with Naked Puts	84
Self-Testing Questions and Exercises		87
	Questions	87

  Exercises 88

10 Trading Strategies with Single Options 89

 10.1 Closing an Option Position by Trading vs Exercising the Option 89
   10.1.1 Selling a Long Option vs Exercising 90
   10.1.2 Buying-to-Close for a Short Option vs Taking Assignment 92
 10.2 Options vs Stock Positions 94
 10.3 Long Options vs Stock Positions 94
   10.3.1 A Long Call vs a Long Stock Position 94
   10.3.2 A Long Put vs a Short Stock Position 96
   10.3.3 Summary of Long Options vs Stock Positions 97
 10.4 Short Options vs Stock Positions 99
   10.4.1 A Short Call vs a Short Stock Position 99
   10.4.2 A Short Put vs a Long Stock Position 100
   10.4.3 Summary of Short Options vs Stock Positions 101
 10.5 Summary of Naked Calls and Puts 105
 Self-Testing Questions and Exercises 106
   Questions 106
   Exercises 107

11 Trend Strategies 109

 11.1 Choosing the Strategy for the Expected Trend 109
 11.2 Long Stock, Long Call, and Short Put 109
 11.3 Short Stock, Short Call, and Long Put 111
 11.4 Summary of Single Options 112
 Self-Testing Questions and Exercises 113
   Questions 113

1 Equities and Derivatives

1.1 Equities and Derivatives

Financial *securities* are any tradable financial instruments including stocks, bonds, options and other financial derivatives, and other assets.

The term *equity* refers to the ownership of a certain asset. The asset may have liabilities including debt, which is deducted from the equity. In the stock market, equity is typically, referred to as shareholder equity that represents the shareholder's ownership in the company. The equity is measured in the amount of money, which the shareholder would own, if the asset is sold and all related liabilities paid off.

A market, where shares of companies' stocks are issued and traded, is referred to as the equity market. Thus, the stock market represents the equity market. The price of stock in the stock market is controlled by demand and supply of the appropriate shares.

Derivatives are financial securities which values are derived from the underlying assets representing equities. Options belong to the category of derivatives. A derivative itself is a contract between two or more parties on buying or selling the underlying asset under predetermined conditions. For this reason, derivative derives its price based on the price of the underlying asset. The derivatives market is the financial market for derivatives –financial instruments like futures contracts or options and other forms of derivatives. The derivatives markets can be divided into two types - exchange-traded derivatives and over-the-counter (OTC) derivatives. The exchange-traded derivatives are listed in the exchanges and traded with market-makers rather than directly between outside traders. The

OTC market operates by matching outside buyers and sellers and typically, us used for unlisted securities.

Thus, one can say, that the company's stock is an abstraction that represents the ownership of the company, while an option is another level of abstraction that represents the company's stock. This hierarchy explains the origin of the term derivative used for stock options.

1.2 Investing in the Stocks Market is Hard Work

Investing in the stock market is an exciting and sophisticated activity with much potential for a gain, but also shows considerable exposure to risk; however, do not treat investing as gambling. You may gain once or twice by boldly taking risk, but be prepared to lose more in the long run if you rely on sheer luck. Success in the stock market comes from a combination of in-depth knowledge of trading techniques, tactics, and strategies; a healthy respect for risk; solid knowledge in stock analysis; thorough understanding of portfolio management, hedging, and optimization; knowledge of current economic and financial realities and perspectives; clear understanding of the investment community and its psychology; a cold-minded character; and, great courage and hard work to put all this together to achieve the investment goals.

1.3 Clearly Understand Your Investment Goal, Financial Capabilities, and Responsibilities

Effective investment is a carefully planned and responsibly managed activity rather than a sporadic hunt for luck.

First of all, you have to clearly understand and unambiguously formulate your investment goals. Your goal could be to generate steady income, grow your wealth, protect your savings from inflation, or something else. No matter what, your goal must be clear.

Secondly, you must clearly realize what amount of money you can safely commit to investing without compromising the wellbeing of your family and other financial obligations. Never invest money from your family budget or special target funds like education, medical expenses, or emergencies.

Financial resources play an essential role in any investment, including stocks. The more resources you put in, the more gains you may expect to get out. You may be tempted to add more funds to your investment by borrowing money or taking it from your family

1 Equities and Derivatives

budget or special purpose savings. Regardless of how promising it looks to take this money and invest it, or to cover a shortage of funds in your existing investment positions for a short time with the expectation of a lucrative return, do not do it. Just DO NOT DO IT! There is no such thing as "no risk" in the stock market, and loss of that money could have devastating consequences to your future.

Do not be greedy. Close your position as soon as it reaches the expected gain. Do not try to squeeze more gains, because odds of the market are strong; you may lose it all. Do not herd heavily losing positions; the situation may turn even worse. Act reasonably.

Self-Testing Questions

1. What are securities?
2. What are equities?
3. What are derivatives?
4. To what extend investment in the stock market is gamble?
5. How important is to clearly understand your investment goals?
6. Can I use my family survival money for the investment in the stock market?

2 The Notion of Options

2.1 Options Basics

Opening long or short stock positions implies certain risk if the stock price takes a "wrong" turn. Such an unfavorable price trend creates losing positions in a portfolio that may result in either a significant loss or in a substantial invested amount of money being frozen, hoping the losing stock position recovers sometime in the future. The bad news is that sometimes, losing positions may never recover.

Definition of Options

An *option* is a contract that gives the holder the right, but not the obligation, to buy or sell a specified quantity of an underlying asset at a predetermined strike price at or before a specified expiration date. After the option expires, the option is no longer valid and becomes worthless.

Underlying assets can be stocks, other securities, or any other investment instruments. In this book, we will focus on stock options, though all major properties of options, except some details, can be easily extended to options of any other underlying assets.

With regard to the stock market, an *option* is a contract that gives the holder the right, but no obligation to buy or sell a specified number of the shares of the underlying stock at a specified strike price on or before a specified expiration date.

An option with the right to buy is referred to as a *call* and an option to sell is referred to as a *put*. A "call" is synonymous with a "call option." Likewise, a "put" is synonymous with a "put option."

Exercising Options, Rights and Obligations

Thus, the option holder (the buyer) has ***the right***, but not the obligation to buy (with a call) or to sell (with a put) a specified number of shares of the underlying stock at a specified strike price on or before the expiration date, while an option seller assumes ***the obligation*** to sell (with call) or to buy (with put) the stocks at the specified strike price, if the corresponding option holder wishes to exercise the option on or before its expiration.

The term *exercise*, as applied to options, means that the option holder can turn the right to buy (with a call) or to sell (with a put) into an action, i.e. to buy the underlying stock at the strike price from the option seller in case of a call and to sell the underlying stock at the strike price to the option seller in case of a put. Note that the option seller has to fulfill his obligation if the option holder wants to exercise the option. If the option holder does not want to exercise the option, the obligation of the option seller terminates with the option expiration.

To summarize the definition of options one can say that the option holder has the right and the option seller assumes the obligation. We have reiterated the definition of options several times because it is very important to clearly understand how options work and what consequences may arise for both the option holder and seller.

Option Expiration

If, for any reason, the option holder has not exercised the option at or before the expiration date, the option expires and is no longer valid. It means that after the expiration the option holder no longer has the right given to him by the option and the option seller becomes free of all obligations related to the option.

American vs. European Options

The options definition given above relates to American options. The European options can be exercised on the expiration day only. Thus,

- American options can be exercised on or before the expiration day.
- European options can be exercised on the expiration day only.

2 The Notion of Options

American options are significantly more flexible than European options. American options allow their holder the possibility of exercising options at the best time, before the expiration, when price is right; while European options are more of a gamble, in that the stock price and expiration date must match.

Options as Derivatives

Options belong to a category of investment instruments referred to as ***derivatives***. In finance, the term derivative applies to a financial contract whose value is derived from the price or performance of the underlying assets. Options, futures, swaps, and other trading instruments belong to the category of derivatives. Accordingly, in the stock market, a derivative is a contract whose value is derived from the price of the underlying stock.

2.2 The Rational for Using Options

Options are traded in exchanges and, hence, can be purchased at market price. An option price is often synonymously referred to as a premium, due to its similarity to insurance payments. The option buyer (holder) pays a premium to buy an option and the option seller receives that premium.

A Call vs. a Long Stock Position

Suppose stock ABA is currently traded at $50 per share. Such a price is referred to as a stock spot price. You expect the stock price to go up, but you are not sure whether the stock price will not drop. If you purchase the stock and the price goes up to $60 per share, you will gain $10 per share, but if the price goes down to $40 per share you will end up with a loss of $10.

Instead of buying a stock, you may buy a call option with a strike price $51 and pay a premium of $2 per option. In this example, we use a strike price, which is different from the spot price, to point out that the strike price and the spot price are two independent parameters of any option.

If the stock price goes up to $60 and you exercise the call and purchase the stock for $51 per share and sell it right away at a spot price of $60. In this example, your gain is $60 - $51 - $2 = $7 per option, excluding commissions.

If the stock price goes down to $40 per share, you just ignore the option and let it expire; in this case, your total loss is $2 per option, which is what you paid for the call option.

A Put vs a Short Stock Position

Suppose stock XYZ is currently traded at a spot price $120 per share. You expect the stock price to decline, but it may go up too. If you open a short stock position by selling the stock short and the stock price goes down to $90 per share, you will gain $30 per share, but if the price rises to $150 per share you will have a loss of $30 per share.

Instead of opening a short position of XYZ, you might want to buy a put option with a strike price $120 and pay a premium of $6 per option.

If the stock price drops to $90, you exercise the put by buying the corresponding number of shares for $90 per share on the market and selling them for $120 per share to those who sold you the put option. This transaction immediately results in a gain of $120 - $90 - $6 = $24 per option excluding commissions.

Another, but similar, transaction of exercising a put may include first selling the stock short at the strike price of $90 per share to those who sold you the put option and then buying the stock to cover at the spot price of $90 on the market to close the short position.

If the stock price rises to $150 per share, you just ignore the put option and let it expire with a total loss of $6 per option, which is only what you paid for the put.

Options are Similar to Insurance

According to the definition of options, they act like insurance. Similar to insurance, one pays a premium and receives protection against losses in case of unfavorable events, i.e. receives the right to claim certain benefits if the specified condition occurs. For instance, the right to receive payment for repairs made to your car damaged in a covered accident. Similar to insurance, the price of an option is also called a premium, which is similar to insurance. Please do not try draw a complete match between options and insurance, but there is enough similarity between their major principles.

2.3 History of Options

2.3.1 Thales of Miletus and Olive Presses

The notion and the use of options go far back into history. Options, in different forms, have been used since ancient times.

Thales of Miletus (c.620 BC – c.546 BC) was one of the most regarded philosophers, mathematician, and astronomers of the ancient Greece. Most information about Thales of Miletus and his achievements have come to us from Aristotle (384 BC – 322 BC). One of Aristotle's stories about Thales concerns olive presses. Once through his analysis, Thales predicted a very good olive harvest. Thales paid olive press owners in his region for the exclusive right to use their presses after the harvest. As predicted by Thales, a great harvest did happen and the demand for olive presses significantly increased. Thales then resold his rights of using the presses and made considerably more money than he had invested.

Thus, Thales created and exercised an option to use the presses. However, if he would have been mistaken, he would lose the money that he paid to the press owners. This money was an option premium. As soon as the bountiful harvest occurred, Thales exercised his option and made a considerable profit.

2.3.2 Options in the Stock Market

Options in the stock market have been known as long as stock exchanges. Brokers and traders sold and bought options over-the-counter (OTC) by broker-dealers who matched option buyers with option sellers. Each option contract was subject to negotiation and possible adjustment to the contract.

Nineteenth century advertisements, for buying and selling options, were published in financial journals and newspapers; thus, establishing the *de facto* option quotation procedure and environment. As the U.S. option community evolved, the Put and Call Brokers and Dealers Association was established as a network of option traders.

In the past, options were not listed on exchanges and were traded exclusively over-the-counter, i.e. in the OTC market. One of the problems of option trading in the past was that, sometimes, it was difficult to enforce the obligation of the option sellers if the option holders were willing to exercise their options, particularly under very unfavorable conditions for the seller.

2.4 Listed Options in the Stock Market

Listed options are options that are listed and traded on the formal stock exchanges. Listed options are the standardized options that can be bought, sold, and exercised, but cannot be changed. Listed options cover underlying securities, such as common stocks,

EFTs, market indices, and commodities. All other options are referred to as **unlisted options**. Listed options are traded on exchanges as securities, in contrast to the unlisted options that are traded over-the-counter (OTC).

The major benefits of exchange-traded options are quick and convenient quotations, the liquidity of the options due to the exchange trading mechanism, and the use of clearinghouses that guarantee option contracts will be fulfilled. Exchange-traded option contracts have been standardized, which makes exchange-traded options easy to buy and sell. The use of clearinghouses enforces the seller's obligations when an option is exercised by the option holder.

Listed standardized options were introduced by the Chicago Board Options Exchange (CBOE) founded in 1973 by the Chicago Board of Trade under name CBOE Holding Inc. CBOE lists and trades standardized options, which could be bought or sold, but not changed. Option trades are cleared by the Option Clearing Corporation (OCC).)

"The Options Clearing Corporation is the sole issuer of all options listed at the CBOE and other U.S. options exchanges, and is the entity through which all CBOE option transactions are ultimately cleared. As the issuer of all options, OCC essentially takes the opposite side of every option traded. Because OCC basically becomes the buyer for every seller and the seller for every buyer, it allows options traders to buy and sell in a secondary market without having to find the original opposite party." [1]

On March 11, 2010, the Chicago Board Options Exchange, as a corporate entity, filed its initial public offering and began trading its shares on Nasdaq under the name CBOE Holding Inc. (Nasdaq: CBOE).

Today, many options are standardized and traded on regulated options exchanges. For each stock, a multitude of standardized options are defined with different strike prices and expiration dates. Figure 2-1 shows a variety of call options for Carnival Corporation &Plc (NYSE: CUK) as of March 20, 2020, with the expiration on May 15, 2020.

---

[1] Retrieved on March 20, 2020 from
http://www.cboe.com/learncenter/concepts/beyond/marketplace.aspx

2 The Notion of Options

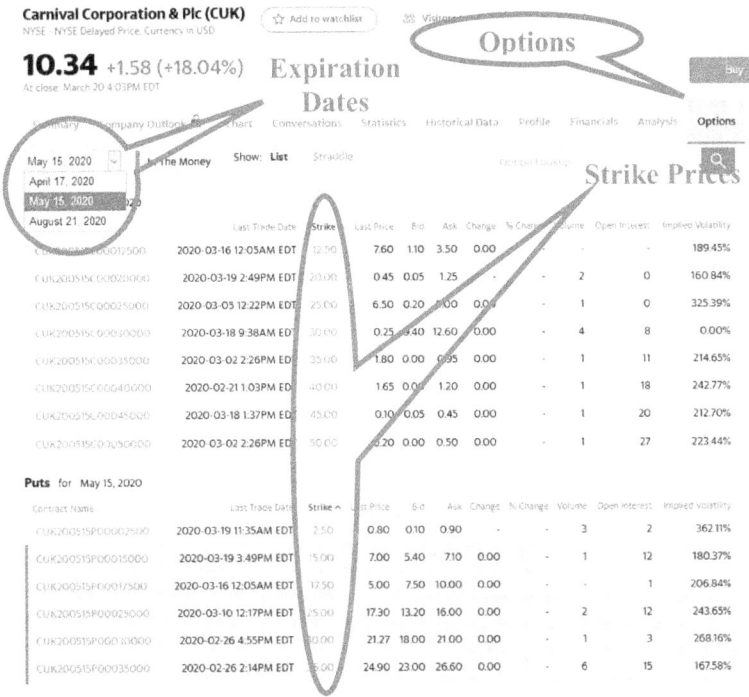

Figure 2-1: A variety of listed call options for Carnival Corporation &Plc (NYSE: CUK) with different strike prices and expiration dates quoted on finance.yahoo.com on March 20, 2020

As it is evident from Figure 2-1, options are defined with a variety of strike prices and expiration dates.

Options are defined in the following format:

[XXX] [ExpirationDate] [StrikePrice] [OptionType]   (2.1)

where [XXX] is the ticker symbol of the underlying security, [ExpirationDate] stands for the expiration date, [StrikePrice] is the strike price, and [OptionType] is the option type, Call or Put. For example, a call option of ABA with the expiration date of September18, 2020, and the strike price of $36 is defined as "ABA September 18 2020 36 Call." A put option of XYZ with the expiration date of July 17, 2020, and the strike price of $10 is defined as "XYZ July17 2020 10 Put."

> An *option,* in general, is a contract that gives the holder the right, but not the obligation to buy or sell the underlying asset (which may include stocks, other securities, or any other investment instruments) at a predetermined strike price at or before a specified expiration date.

> In the stock market, an *option* is a contract that gives the holder the right, but not the obligation to buy or sell a specified quantity of the underlying stock at a predetermined strike price on or before a specified expiration date.
> - **Call** is an option to buy
> - **Put** is an option to sell

> An option holder (the buyer) has the right, but not the obligation to buy (with a Call) or to sell (with a Put); but, an option seller assumes the obligation to sell (with a Call) or to buy (with a Put), if the corresponding option holder decides to exercise the option before or at its expiration.

Self-Testing Questions

1. What is an option and how does it work?
2. What rights and obligations do the buyer (holder) and the seller of the option have?
3. What is the strike price and expiration date of an option?
4. Why is an option market price referred to as a premium?
5. What is the difference between Call and Put options?
6. What is the difference between listed and unlisted options?

3 Intrinsic and Extrinsic Values of Options

3.1 Two Components of Options Value

Options are traded on exchanges and their prices (premiums) are based on demand and supply, similarly to any other tradable asset. An option price is partially derived from the price of the underlying stock, versus the option strike price, and partially from gain opportunities, due to the uncertainty in the underlying stock price in the future before the option expiration.

Thus the market value of an option consists of two components:
- Intrinsic value
- Extrinsic or time value

The ***intrinsic value*** of an option is derived from the spot price of the underlying stock while the ***extrinsic*** or the ***time value*** of the option depends on the time left until its expiration and represents the opportunity component of the option. The terms "***extrinsic value***" and "***time value***" are synonymous.

Thus, the total value, V, of an option can be expressed as a sum of the intrinsic and the time (extrinsic) values of the option as

$$V = V_{Intr} + V_{Time} \qquad (3.1)$$

where V_{Intr} is the intrinsic value and V_{Time} is the extrinsic (time) value of the option.

3.2 Intrinsic Value of Options

The *intrinsic value* of an option is the gain, which the trader can get, if exercises the option right now. This gain depends on the option strike price and the spot price of the underlying stock.

The intrinsic value of an option V_{Intr} is defined as following:

$$\text{for a Call: } V_{Intr} = \max(P-K, 0)$$
$$\text{for a Put : } V_{Intr} = \max(K-P, 0) \quad (3.2)$$

where K is the option strike price and P is the price of the underlying stock. The intrinsic value of a call, is $P - K$ if the spot stock price P is greater than the strike price K, i.e. if $P > K$, otherwise the intrinsic value is zero. The intrinsic value of a put is $K - P$ if the spot stock price P is lower than the strike price K, i.e. if $P < K$, otherwise the intrinsic value of the put is zero.

The intrinsic value of an option depends only on the strike price and the spot price of the underlying stock. Figure 3-1 shows the intrinsic value for call and put options.

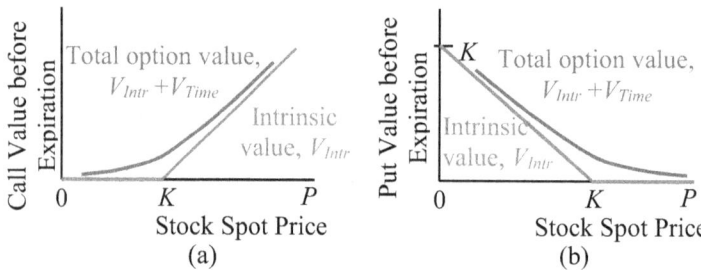

Figure 3-1: Intrinsic (the Red solid line) and total value (the Blue solid Line) of an option: (a) for a call and (b) for a put as a function of the underlying stock price. K is the option strike price

If the intrinsic value of an option is positive, then the option is referred to as being *in-the-money* (ITM). For a call, it means that the price of the underlying stock is greater than the strike price; while, for a put, it means that the price of the underlying stock is lower than the strike price.

3 Intrinsic and Extrinsic Values of Options

An option is referred to as being **out-of-the-money** (OTM)[2] if, for a call, the price of the underlying stock is lower than the strike price; while, for a put, the price of the underlying stock is greater than the put strike price. It means that the intrinsic value of the option equals zero, i.e. exercising the option makes no sense.

An option is **at-the-money** (ATM) when the strike price of an option equals the current price of the underlying stock. Being at-the-money is a quite an infrequent borderline situation between being in-the-money and out-of-the-money. The intrinsic value for an option being at-the-money is zero, so exercising an option at-the-money also makes no sense, which is similar to the out-of-the-money option.

Being in-the-money, means that the option would generate profit if exercised and the resulting stock position—a long position for exercising a call and a short position for exercising a put—is immediately closed at the market spot price. Neither the premium paid for the option nor any transaction commissions are included in the calculation of intrinsic value.

If a call is out-of-the-money, then it would be cheaper to buy the underlying stock at the market price than to exercise the call because $P < K$. If a put is out-of-the-money, then the put holder would better off selling the underlying stock at the market price than to exercise the option because $P > K$.

Intrinsic value of an option V_{Intr} is defined as following:
for a Call: $V_{Intr} = \max(P - K, 0)$
for a Put : $V_{Intr} = \max(K - P, 0)$
where K is the option strike price and P is the price of the underlying stock.

- The term being **in-the-money** (ITM) is used to identify calls with $P > K$ and puts with $P < K$, i.e. for the options with a positive intrinsic value
- The term being **at-the-money** (ATM) is used to identify options with $P = K$. The ATM options have zero intrinsic value.

---

[2] The term **out-of-money** is often used in the financial markets as a synonym of **out-of-the-money**.

> • The term being *out-of-the-money* (**OTM**)) is used to identify calls with $P < K$ and puts with $P > K$. The OTM options have zero intrinsic value.

Example 1

The current spot price (current market price) of ABA stock on June 12, 2020, is $P = \$120.02$.
- The call "APA June 19 2020 115 Call" has the strike price $K = \$115.00$ and is in-the-money by $P - K = \$120.02 - 115.00 = \$5.02$.
- The call "APA June 19 2020 130 Call" has the strike price $K = \$130.00$ and is out-of-the-money because $P < K$.

Example 2

The current spot price of XYZ stock on June 9, 2020, is $P = \$100.00$.
- The put "XYZ June 19 2020 95 Put" has the strike price $K = \$95.00$ and is out-of-the-money because $P > K$.
- The put "XYZ June 19 2020 XYZ June 19 2020 120 Put" has the strike price $K = \$120.00$ and is in-the-money by $K - P = \$120.00 - 100.00 = \$20$.
- The put "XYZ June 19 2020 100 Put" has the strike price $K = \$100.00$ and is at-the-money because $K = P$.

3.3   Extrinsic or Time Value of Options

Time Value of an Option

The option premium (price) goes beyond the intrinsic value. Suppose an option strike price is equal to the underlying stock spot price, i.e. $K = P$, that is, the option is at-the-money and its intrinsic value is zero. Even with zero intrinsic value, the option still has a positive market value because there is a chance that the underlying stock price will change over time and the option will become in-the-money before its expiration. The underlying stock price may evolve in the right direction and bring more value to the options before its expiration, which are currently: out-of-the money, at-the-money, or even in-the-money. Such opportunities of a possible gain before the option expires increases the option's value above the their intrinsic value as indicated in Eq.(3.1). This additional value is referred to as

3 Intrinsic and Extrinsic Values of Options

the *extrinsic value* or the *time value* of an option equation. The terms time value and extrinsic value are synonyms. The time value (extrinsic value) for an option, V_{Time}, can be also defined as an amount by which the current market price (premium) of an option, V, exceeds its intrinsic value, V_{Intr}, i.e.

$$V_{Time} = V - V_{Intr} \tag{3.3}$$

which is actually identical to Eq.(3.1). Thus, the time value (extrinsic value) of an option is the additional value of the option associated with the additional gain opportunities given by the potential stock price variations till the option expiration.

Arithmetically, Eq.(3.3) and Eq.(3.1) are identical, but, logically, Eq.(3.3) says that the option intrinsic value V_{Intr} is calculated from the strike price and the spot price of the underlying stock and the option market price, V, comes from the market, while the option time (extrinsic) value is derived as the difference between the option market price and its intrinsic value. Thus, one can calculate the extrinsic value from the known intrinsic and market values.

Dependence of an Option Time Value on Stock and Strike Prices

The analysis of Eq.(3.3) and Figure 3-1 shows that an option time value depends on the option strike price and the price of the underlying stock as shown in Figure 3-2.

As is evident from Figure 3-2, option time value symmetrically depends on the distance between the underlying stock spot price and the option strike price, with the highest time value for the option with the strike price equal to the price of the underlying stock. The options with the strike prices farther from the underlying stock price have lower time value. The farther the option strike price is from the spot price of the underlying stock, the lower the time value of the option.

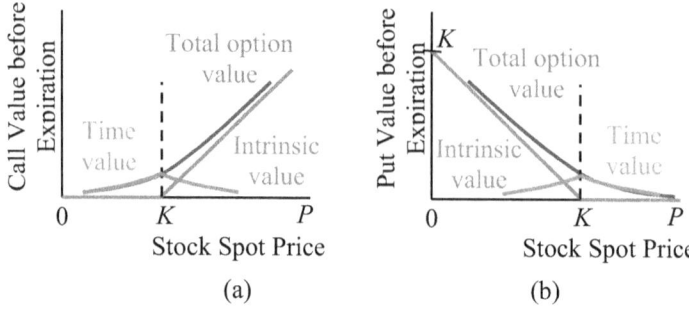

Figure 3-2: Option time value as a function of the underlying stock price P and the strike price K: (a) for a call and (b) for a put. The time value is shown with a Green line.

Similarly, one can conclude that an option with the strike price closer to the spot price of the underlying stock has the highest time value of all similar options with the strike prices farther from the underlying stock spot price as shown in Figure 3-3.

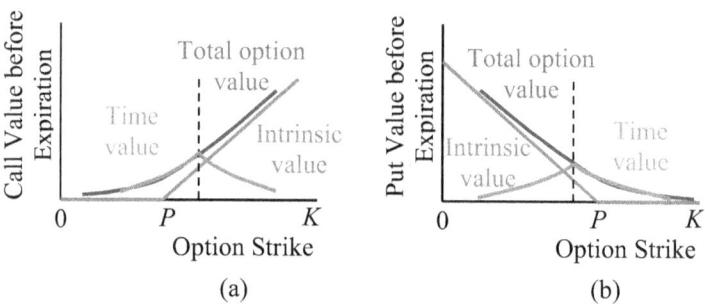

Figure 3-3: Option time value as a function of the strike price K and the underlying stock spot price P: (a) for a call and (b) for a put. The time value is shown with a Green line.

Figure 3-3 is identical to Figure 3-2, but presents a different perspective. An interesting feature of the option time value can be derived from its dependence on the distance between the strike price

3 Intrinsic and Extrinsic Values of Options

and the underlying stock spot price. The options time value may vary as the price of the underlying stock changes over time and the options with the strike prices closer to the current spot price of the underlying stock exhibit the highest time value. This feature plays a significant role in selecting trading strategies with options, which we will discuss in the next two chapters.

Dependence of an Option Time Value on the Time till Expiration

Figure 3-4(a) shows the time value of options, both calls and puts, for First Solar, Inc. (Nasdaq: FSLR) at different strike prices as a function of the underlying stock price. The data were recorded on June 25, 2020, at the time when the FSLR stock price $P = \$50.00$. Note that the strike prices for options were actually varying by increments of 5.

Time Value of Calls and Puts

In a stable market, an option's time value is expected to be a symmetrical function of the distance between the option's strike price and the underlying stock's price. Such a symmetrical pattern is shown in Figure 3-4.

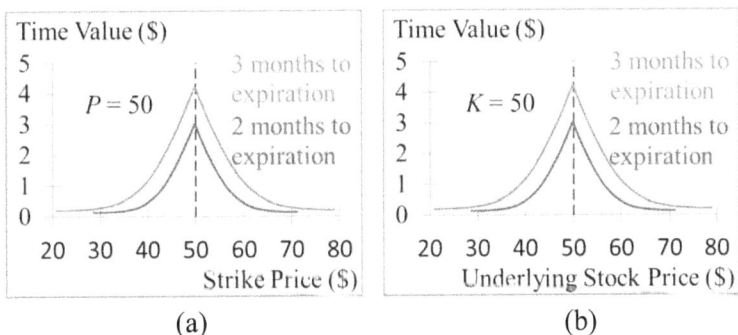

Figure 3-4: Options (calls and puts) time value for First Solar, Inc. (Nasdaq: FSLR) on June 25, 2020, with the expiration on August 21, 2020, (the Green curve) and September 18, 2020, (the Red curve): (a) as a function of the strike price K with a fixed underlying stock price P and (b) as a function of the underlying stock price P with a fixed strike price K

The option, whose strike price is equal to the underlying stock's spot price, has the highest time value among all options of the underlying stock that have the same expiration date. The time value of the options, with the same expiration date, decreases as the distance between the underlying stock's price and the option's strike price grows, regardless of the direction, i.e. whether the strike price is higher or lower than the stock's price (Figure 3-4).

The time value of a call and a put for the same underlying stock, having the same strike price and the same expiration date, are expected to be equal in a balanced and stable market condition when the expectation for the underlying stock's price is neutral, i.e. the price is equally expected to increase and to decrease. This was illustrated in Figure 3-4, which represents time values for calls and puts.

Such behavior can be explained by the nature of time value, which represents uncertainty in the possible changes of the underlying stock's prices. If the stock is stable, its spot price reflects all known information about the stock and its possible price variations, which, ideally, are equal in both directions. However, if the stock's price shows strong trend momentum due to market fluctuations or a biased expectation, the time value symmetry may not occur.

Time Decay of the Option Time (Extrinsic) Value

As is evident from Figure 3-4, the options time value is higher for the option with the longer time till expiration.

Extrinsic or time value of an option reflects the opportunities that may come with the changes of the underlying stock's price over time. The longer time left till expiration, the more opportunities the option presents to investors. This means that, with the longer time till expiration, more chances are that significant changes in the underlying stock price may occur, which will result in a better gain with the option. However, the closer the expiration date, the fewer opportunities may be expected. The shorter the time before the expiration, the fewer the opportunities that can be expected; therefore, the option price becomes equal to the option intrinsic value. The time value of any option drops to zero as its expiration date approaches. A typical course of time decay of the option time (extrinsic) value is shown in Figure 3-5.

3 Intrinsic and Extrinsic Values of Options

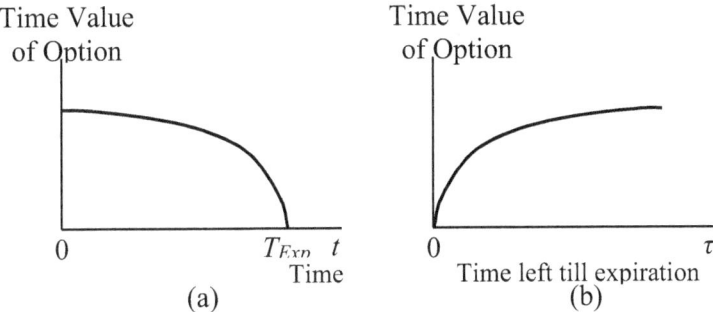

Figure 3-5: Time value decay of an option as a function of: (a) time where $T_{\exp}$ is the expiration date and (b) time τ left till the expiration

Figure 3-5(a) shows the time decay of the extrinsic (time) value of an option as a function of time where t_{Exp} is the option expiration date. Figure 3-5(b) shows the time decay of the extrinsic (time) value of an option as a function of the time left to the expiration. Both graphs are completely identical and represent just different views of the same thing. The closer to the expiration, the steeper the time value decay. Both types of options, calls and puts, show a similar (but not identical) pattern of time decay of the extrinsic value.

The option time value decay shown in Figure 3-5 does not take into account for changes of the price of the underlying stock's price over time till option expiration. The closer the underlying stock price to the option strike price, the higher is the time value as indicated in Figure 3-4. Thus, the time value of an option may temporarily increase due to the decreasing difference between the underlying stock and strike prices or more rapidly drop due to the increasing distance between the underlying stock and strike prices. This effect may cause a temporary increase of the option time value over time, or a temporary drop, but, finally, the time value of any option falls to zero at its expiration. The effect of price variation of the underlying stock on the time value of an option is illustrated in Figure 3-6.

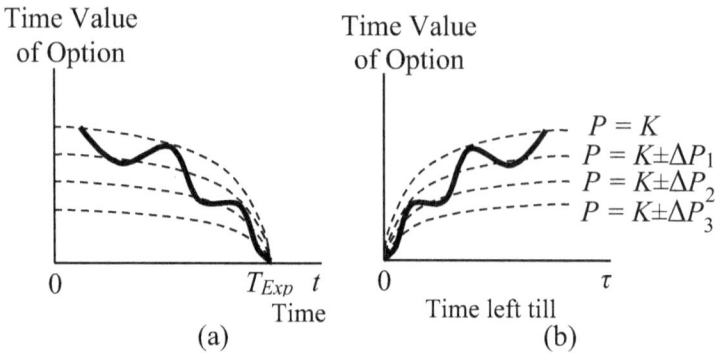

Figure 3-6: Dependence of the time value decay of an option on the price variation of the underlying stock as a function of: (a) time where T_{exp} is the expiration date and (b) time τ left till the expiration

Four dashed decay curves in each section of Figure 3-6 show the time value decay curves for an option with a strike price, K, for different prices, P, of the underlying stock. The upper curve is for $P = K$ and the lower decay curves are for the prices deviating from the option strike price by $|\Delta P_1| < |\Delta P_2| < |\Delta P_3|$. The option time value switches between different decay curves as the price of the underlying stock changes over time.

Example 3

The current spot price of ABA stock is $P = \$112.25$ on March 11, 2020. A call "AAPL May 8 2020 110 Call," with the strike price $K = \$110.00$, is $P - K = \$112.25 - \$110.00 = \$2.25$. The market price paid for the call is $V = \$5.72$ per call. According to Eq.(3.3) the time value of the call equals the difference between the market price and the intrinsic value of the option, i.e. $V_{Time} = V - V_{Intr} = \$5.72 - \$2.25 = \$3.50$.

As of May 20, 2020, the APA stock price was $P = \$109.83$. Hence, the call was out-of-the-money because the stock price $P = \$109.83$ was lower than the strike price $K = \$110.00$, hence, the intrinsic value of the call was $V_{Intr} = 0$. The market price of the call was $V = \$2.92$.

3 Intrinsic and Extrinsic Values of Options

The closing price[3] of APA stock was $P_{Exp} = \$121$ on May 8, 2020, (the call expiration). The time value of the option at the expiration was zero, $V_{Time} = 0$, and the intrinsic value of the call was $V_{Intr} = P_{Exp} - K = \$121.06 - \$110.00 = \$11.06$. The total value of the call at the expiration was $V_{Intr} + V_{Time} = \$11.06 + \$0 = \$11.06$.

Example 4

The price (premium) for a put of XYZ, with the strike price $92 and expiration on April 24, 2020, i.e. "XYZ April 24 2020 92 Put" was $V = \$3.30$ per put on March 20, 2020. The then current spot price of XYZ stock was $91.27. The intrinsic value of the option on the same day was $92.00 - $91.37 = $0.63 and the time value of the option was $3.30 - $0.63 = $2.67.

The stock price of XYZ at the market close on the expiration day, April 24, 2020, was $P = \$100.29$. The time value of the put was zero, $V_{Time} = \$0$, at the expiration because the time value of any option is always zero at the expiration. The intrinsic value of the put was zero too, $V_{Intr} = \$0$, according to Eq.(3.2) because the stock price P was higher than the strike price K. Thus, the put expired worthless.

Extrinsic value or **time value** of an option reflects the opportunities that may come with the changes of the underlying stock price over time. The longer time left till expiration, the more opportunities the option presents to investors.

$$V_{Time} = V - V_{Intr}$$

where V_{Time} is the intrinsic value, C is the option premium (the option market price), and V_{Intr} is the intrinsic value of the option.

---

[3] "Closing price" refers to the last price at which a stock trades during a regular trading session

Self-Testing Questions and Exercises

Questions

1. What is the meaning of the terms trading "volume" and "open interest" for options?
2. What types of values constitute the value of an option?
3. What are the intrinsic and extrinsic values of an option?
4. How is the intrinsic value of an option calculated?
5. How do extrinsic and intrinsic values of an option depend on the time till expiration?
6. What is the difference between extrinsic and time value of an option?
7. How does time value of an option depend on time before the expiration?
8. Can the option time value grow over time?
9. How big can the extrinsic value of an option be just before the expiration?
10. What are the meanings of the terms "in-the-money," "out-of-the-money," and "at-the money" in options?

Exercises

1. Stock ABA is currently traded at a spot price of $38.00. What is the intrinsic value of a call option with the strike price $35.00?
2. Stock ABA is currently traded at a spot price of $38.00. What is the extrinsic (time) value of a call option with the strike price $35.00, if the premium for the call is $4.12?
3. A put with the strike price of $26 has an intrinsic value of $2.80. What is the current spot price of the underlying stock?
4. Stock XYZ is now traded at $42.00 per share. What are the intrinsic values of a call and a put options, both with strike prices of $40.00?
5. A call with the strike price of $29.00 and the expiration date in two weeks is traded at $3.21 per call. The underlying stock is traded at $30.17 per share. What is the time value of the call?

4 Options Trading

4.1 The Size of Stock Options Market

Options belong to category of derivatives. According to CME Group[4] and other market research firms, the world's derivatives market is estimated about $700 trillion - $1.2 quadrillion[5] in 2019. It is hard or even impossible to provide an accurate estimate of this market due to lack of actual information. However, even such estimates clearly show that the size of derivative market is in order of magnitude higher than the global world GDP.

On one hand, the size of the derivative market indicates a huge interest in derivatives, but on the other side, raises a "red flag" of possible problems in the global economy, which could be triggered by this loosely controlled market.

4.2 Option Contracts and Quotation

Options are traded by *contracts*. Each *contract* includes 100 identical options. So, if you buy 1 contract, it means that you buy 100 options, 2 contracts mean 200 options, and so on. Listed options are traded as securities, i.e. in an auction style on the public exchanges, and their market prices depend on demand and supply.

An option quotation is, to a degree, similarly to a stock quotation. The format of the option quotation consists of the option

---

[4] CME Group Inc. – Chicago Mercantile Exchange & Chicago Board of Trade is one of the largest options and futures exchanges: www.cmegroup.com

[5] 1 quadrillion = 10^5

definition with its bid and ask prices. The option definition includes the underlying stock ticker symbol, expiration date, strike price, and the option type which can be call or put.

As was mentioned above, there could be a broad variety of options for each underlying stock as shown in Figure 2-1 for TSLA calls and Figure 4-1 for TSLA puts with different strike prices and different expiration dates. The same figures show the market quotation for each option.

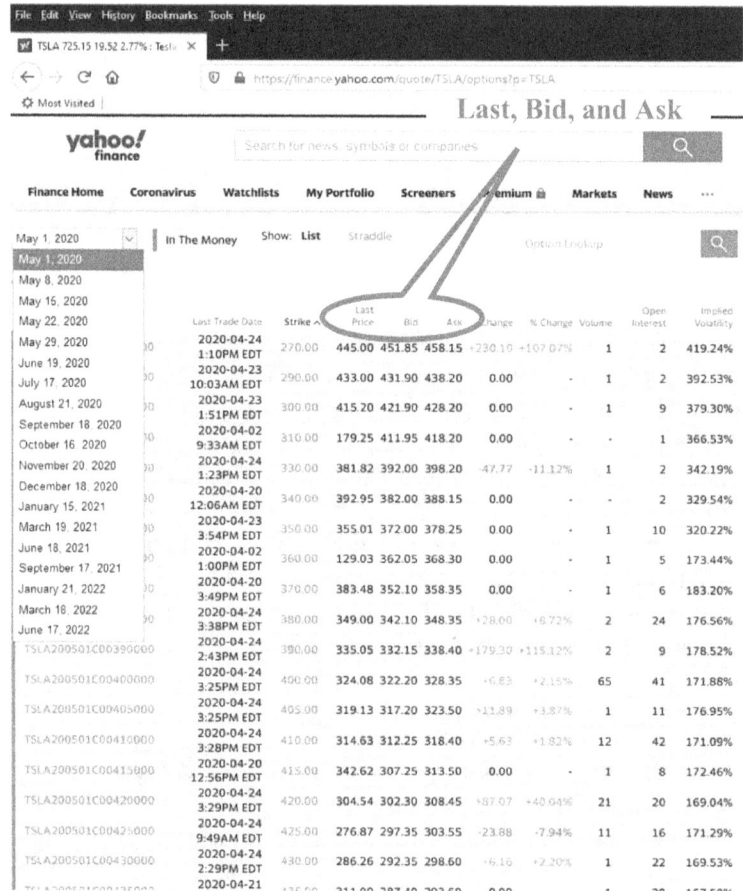

Figure 4-1: A variety of listed put options for Tesla Motors, Inc. (Nasdaq: TSLA) with different strike prices and expiration dates quoted on finance.yahoo.com

Please keep in mind that in any market transaction with options, including trading or exercise, traders are dealing with

4 Options Trading

contracts, each contract consists of 100 options, so all costs[6] and gains for one option should be multiplied by 100 to represent one contract.

If a trader wants to buy or sell 200 options they have to buy or sell 2 contracts, for 500 options, they will buy or sell 5 contracts. The number of contracts has to be integer, so there is no way a trader can buy or sell 260 or 726 options. The number of contracts should be an integer that includes the number of options in multiples of 100.

Example 5

The following quotation "ABA June 20 2020 235 Call 23.25 25.85" means that a call option of ABA with the expiration date on June 20, 2020, and the strike price $K = \$235.00$ has a bid price equal $23.25 and an ask price equals $25.85 per option. Thus, if you want to buy one contract it will cost you $25.85*100 = \$2,585$.

Example 6

The following quotation "XYZ June 20 2020 270 Put 29.80 32.85" means that a put option of XYZ with an expiration date of June 20, 2020 and the strike price $K = \$270.00$ has the bid price equal $29.80 and the ask price equals 32.85 per option. If you want to sell two contracts, you will receive $29.80*200 = \$5,960$ minus commissions.

> Options are traded by **contracts**, 100 identical options per one contract.

The liquidity of listed options, traded on exchanges, has dramatically changed option trading strategies and habits. With exchange-traded options, investors no longer build their strategies on only exercising the successful or ignoring the failing options, but also on reselling options as their market price changes favorably. Typically, exchange-traded options will change hands several times before expiring.

---

[6] Option trading commissions may be charged by the brokerage firms by contract rather than by option.

4.3 Who Makes Options

Shares of listed stocks appear on the appropriate exchange through the IPO (Initial Public Offering) or SPO (Secondary Public Offering) procedures forming the float traded on the exchange. Thus, the quantity of shares of each stock available for trading on an exchange does not change unless the company conducts an SPO or repurchases (buys back) its own stock.

In contrast to stocks, listed options are first defined, but not yet actually issued until someone buys the first contract of the option. To buy the first contract of a given option, it is necessary that someone would sell such a yet physically nonexistent contract. Thus, for a trader who wants to buy a specific option, a match with a party should be found that wants to sell such an option, i.e. to assume the obligation part of the sold contract. The role of the option seller can be played by another trader or by OCC to maintain options liquidity.

Terms for listed options are non-negotiable by the parties, therefore the buyer and seller must choose from a list of predefined options listed on the exchange. A variety of options defined and listed on the exchanges for each stock are different by their strike price and expiration dates. Thus, as the first buy-sell transaction occurs for a listed option, new physical instances of that option are created. Therefore, the term *write* an option contract means selling a newly created option contract. This action is also referred to as *selling short* an option contract. The terms *write* an option contract and *sell short* an option contract are synonymous and imply creating new instances of the option. Writing (or selling short) one option contract adds one count to the number of the existing instances of the options of the given type, one count per one contract. The count on the currently existing instances of the given option is referred to as *open interest*. Later, someone who holds options may resell the existing option contracts to another trader. Such a transaction does not change the number of actually existing instances of the option contracts of that given type and hence the count of open interest does not change. Selling options, which the seller does not have, i.e. writing the options (or selling options short), works differently from selling short shares of the stock. In a short sale of a stock, the trader has first to borrow the shares of the stock from the broker and then sell the shares while selling options, which the trader does not have, thereby creating a new instance or instances of the listed options. If a trader sells options that he currently holds, then such a transaction does not create new instances of the option because those instances of the option already exist.

If a trader, who holds a short position of an option, buys a similar option from the market, the existing short and the new long positions may get mutually liquidated and those instances of the option cease to exist on the market, decreasing the open interest for this option by one count for each contract.

> Instances of listed options are dynamically created and cancelled in the process of trading on the exchange.

> The count on the currently existing instances of the given option is referred to as *open interest*.

The bottom line is that open interest for any given option may dynamically change due to option trading. This may sound confusing at first glance, but after some contemplation, it should become clear.

4.4 Trading Actions

Listed options are traded on exchanges like securities. Traders can open and close long and short option positions by conducting the following trading activities, which are discussed in detail below:
- buy-to-open
- sell-to-close
- sell-to-open
- buy-to-close

Buy-to-Open

The *buy-to-open* action for options is similar to the *buy* action for stocks. With this action, a trader creates a new or expands an existing long position of the option. A long option position means that the trader holds the option, i.e. the trader has the right to buy the underlying stock at the strike price at or before the expiration in case of a call or has the right to sell the underlying stock at the strike price at or before the expiration in case of a put. *Buy-to-open* does not necessary create new instances or liquidate the existing instance of the option and, hence, does not change the option interest.

Sell-to-Close

The **sell-to-close** trading action is used to close or reduce an existing long option position. **Sell-to-close** does not necessarily create new instances or liquidate existing instances of the option and, hence, does not change the option interest.

Sell-to-Open

The **sell-to-open** trading action for options opens or expands a short option position by creating a new instance(s) of the options subject to the number of traded contracts. This action creates new instances of the option of the specified type on the exchange and, hence, increases the count of open interest by the number of traded contracts. This action results in a "short" option position. Opening a short option position implies the obligation assumed by the option seller to fulfill the right of the option holder if the option holder decides to exercise the right given to him by the option. A "short" option position is not the same as a short stock position. A "short" option position does not imply borrowing of options but initiates creation of a new instance(s) of the option.

Please note that **sell-to-open** does not close a long option position if the seller previously had a long position of that option. To close the existing long position, the holder has to use a sell-to-close action.

Buy-to-Close

The **buy-to-close** trading action for options is used to close a short option position fully or partially, subject to the number of traded contracts. By closing short positions with this action, the appropriate number of the option instances are liquidated, i.e. cease to exist, and the count of open interest goes down by the number of closed contracts for the given option.

This action does not create a long option position and is used exclusively for fully or partially closing existing short option positions. To create a long option position, the buyer has to use buy-to-open trading action.

Thus, "buy-to-open" and "sell-to-close" do not change the number of the existing instances of the option keeping the open interest unchanged. Action "sell-to-open" results in the creation of additional instances of the option, increasing the open interest by one per each contract. Action "buy-to-close" results in the reduction of one existing instances of the option, decreasing the open interest by one per each contract.

4.5 Dimensions of Option Trading Orders

An option trading order includes the option description, the trading action, the number of contracts, and other trading parameters similar to those for the stock trading orders.
The option description includes the following parameters:
- underlying stock
- option type: Call or Put
- option strike price
- option expiration

The trading action includes:
- order action: Buy-to-Open, sell-to-close, sell-to-open, and Buy-to-Close
- number of contracts

and the order parameters similar to stock orders as:
- execution price: Market or Limit
- activation conditions: Stop, Trailing Stop
- order timing: Day, GTC
- special instructions: All or None, Fill or Kill
- order routing

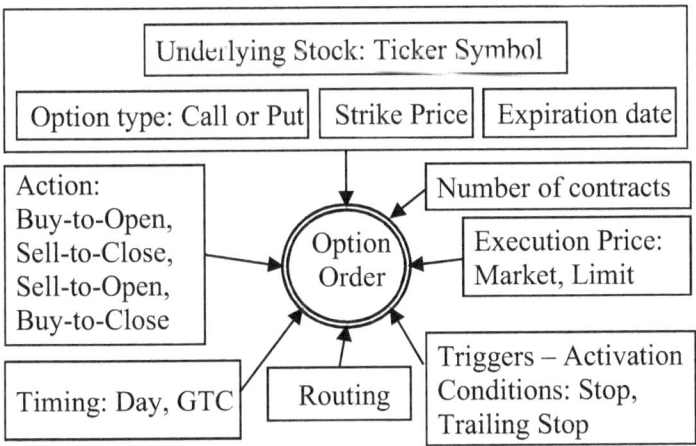

Figure 4-2: Dimensions of an option order

You probably noticed that the order timing for options does not include extended hours as it was for trading stocks. Options are traded only during official trading hours and are not traded when the market is closed.

The parameters (which we call dimensions) of an option order are shown in Figure 4-2.[7]

4.6 Option Exercise and Assignment

How Options are Exercised and Assigned

If an option holder decides to exercise the rights given by the option, the option seller has the obligation to fulfill the option exercise request. The option seller has to meet the obligation to sell the underlying stock to the option holder at the strike price in case of a call or to buy the underlying stock from the option holder at the strike price in case of a put. This action for the option holder is referred to as **option exercise** and for the option seller is referred to as **option assignment**. Thus, if the option holder decides to exercise the option, the option seller receives the option assignment.

Option exercise brings to the option holder the intrinsic value of the option and, hence, should take place only if the option is in-the-money; otherwise exercising the option makes no sense due to its zero intrinsic value.

In a call assignment, the call seller has the obligation to sell the underlying stock to the option holder at the strike price, one share of the stock per one option, which means hundred shares of the stock per one option contract. If the seller does not have the shares of underlying stock available, the seller is obligated to buy them on the open market to fulfill the assignment or to open a short position of the underlying stock.

In case of a put assignment, the option seller has the obligation to buy the underlying stock from the option holder at the strike price, again, one hundred shares of the underlying stock per one option contract. There are three scenarios for exercising a put. If the put holder has a long position of the underlying stock with the sufficient number of shares, then the required number of shares will be sold to the assigned put seller from this long position. If the put holder does not have a long position of the underlying stock or does

---

[7] For more information about each dimension of trading, please refer to the complete course "Stock Market Course, Part 1: Stock exchanges, Stocks, and Options." (2020)

not have a sufficient number of shares in the long position of the underlying stock, then the put holder opens a short position of the underlying stock. However, it may occur that the shares of the underlying stock are not available at the brokerage company for short sale. In this case, the put holder can buy the shares of the underlying stock on the market and then sell the shares to the assigned put seller.

Automatic Option Exercise and Assignment

The option holder can initiate the option exercise any time before or at the option expiration. According to the OCC rule, all options that are $0.01 or more in-the-money at their expiration are automatically exercised even if the options holder does not initiate the exercise. This rule provides a convenient closure to expiring in-the-money options.

However, it may occur that the intrinsic value of an "in-the-money" option at expiration is lower than the commissions charged for the option exercise. This may result, in some cases, to a small loss for both the option holder and the option seller. Suppose an option holder has one contract of options expiring with $0.01 in-the-money. According to the OCC automatic exercise rule, the options are automatically exercised upon the expiration at the strike price with the gain of $0.01 * 100 = $1.00 per contract. However, the option exercise commissions are typically much higher than $1.00. Thus, the option holder ends up with a loss, not a significant loss, but still a loss. At the same time, the option seller is assigned the options and has to pay $0.01 * 100 = $1.00 to the option holder, which is equal to the option intrinsic value at the expiration. However, the option seller has to pay an assignment commission too, which increases the loss. Under the circumstances, when an option is just $0.01 or is relatively low in-the-money at expiration, both parties, the option holder and the option seller, would most likely prefer to discard the option without exercising it. However, the option holder can prevent the automatic option exercise if needed.

The intrinsic value of an option at its expiration is recorded according to the closing price of the underlying stock on the expiration date. This is the price of the last trade of the underlying stock during regular trading hours, i.e. at 4:00 PM EST (1:00 PM PST), except on certain days when the market closes earlier. After market close, the option holder still has a couple of hours to call the brokerage company to give an instruction not to exercise the option, if the option exercise is not profitable because of the commissions. The option seller, on the other hand, does not have such a choice. OCC randomly assigns in-the-money options to the option sellers upon expiration.

4.7 Volume and Open Interest

Volume

Trading volume is a measure that counts all trading transactions with the options over the period of time. Typically it could be daily, monthly or annual volume.

In general, volume is an important indicator of trading activity. High average trading volume indicates high interest of traders in the security, while low average trading volume shows low interest in the security. A daily stock trading **volume** is calculated as a number of shares traded in one trading day.

Similarly, daily option trading volume is calculated as the number of option contracts of a given type traded in one trading day. Just a reminder, options are traded by contracts, 100 options in each contract. Suppose, call options of ABA with a strike price $30 and an expiration day on June 19, 2020 (ABA June 19 2020 30 Call), were traded with the volume of 1,705 contracts on the trading day of April 23, 2020. It means that 1,705*100 = 170,500 "INTC June 19, 2020 30 Call" options were traded by those 1,705 contracts on that day.

Please do not get confused with a relatively low trading volume in the example above; options are normally traded in much lower volumes than stocks; this occurs due to a broad variety of options for each underlying stock, rather than due to low interest from traders. The above volume is relatively high for an option.

Open Interest

Open interest is another important parameter for option trading that shows the number of the currently existing instances of contracts for the given options. As was discussed above, the total number of existing options on an exchange dynamically changes during the course of trading. The trading action "sell-to-open" creates new instances of option contracts and the action "buy-to-close" removes the specified number of the option contracts from the market. Also, option exercise/assignment removes the appropriate number of options from the market and, hence, from count of open interest, one count per option contract.

The Summary of Option Volume and Open Interest

Option trading volume counts all trading transactions with the given options that took place during a given period, but does not count option exercise and assignment transactions. The volume during one trading day is referred to as daily volume.

The option open interest counts the number of the existing contracts of the given option. This count increases only with a "sell-to-open" action, equal to the number of contracts in the transaction. The open interest count decreases either with a "buy-to-close" action, equal to the number of contracts in the transaction or with option exercise by the number of exercised options.

To better understand the meaning of open interest and volume, let's go through the following example.

Example 7

Suppose a call option of the XYZ stock, with a given expiration date, and a given strike price has just been listed on the exchange "XYZ Expiration Date Strike Price Call." At the beginning of the trading day, no instances of this kind of option existed and its open interest equaled zero. To illustrate this, imaginary trading of the option with its volume and open interest is presented in Table 4-1.

In Table 4-1, columns "Trader" for the seller and for the buyer identify the traders by showing their names. Column "Action" shows the trading action, where BO stands for buy-to-open, SC stands for sell-to-close, SO stands for sell-to-open, BC stands for buy-to-close, and EX stands for option exercise. Column "# Traded Contracts" shows the number of contracts traded in the transaction. Columns, "Volume," and "Open Interest" show trading volume and open interest, respectively. Columns in "Resultant # of Contracts in Traders' Hands" show the resultant number of contracts in hand for each trader after the transaction.

It is presumed that no instances of the option contracts existed before the first transaction, i.e. the open interest was equal to zero and trading volume was equal to zero.

In transaction #1, trader A sold-to-open (SO) 2 contracts to trader B, who bought-to-open (BO). In this transaction, 2 new option contracts were created by the sell-to-open (SO) action. As a result, the volume was 2 and the open interest was 2.

Table 4-1: Imaginary trading volume and open interest for "XYZ Expiration Date Strike Price Call" (BO stands for buy-to-open, SC stands for sell-to-close, SO stands for sell-to-open, BC stands for buy-to-close), and EX stands for option exercise. The actions resulted in changes in open interest are highlighted for clarity.

Transaction	Seller Trader	Seller Action	Buyer Trader	Buyer Action	#Traded	Volume	Open Interest	Contracts in Traders' Hands A	Contracts in Traders' Hands B	Contracts in Traders' Hands C	Comment
1	A	SO	B	BO	2	2	2	-2	2	0	2 contracts were traded, 2 new contracts created by sell-to-open (SO). Volume and open interest added 2 each.
2	B	SC	C	BO	1	3	2	-2	1	1	1 contract was traded sell-to-close (SC), buy-to-open (BO), so new contracts were neither created nor liquidated. Volume increased by 1, open interest stayed unchanged.
3	B	SC	A	BC	1	4	1	-1	0	1	1 contract traded and 1 contract liquidated by the buy-to-close (BC). Volume increased by 1 but open interest decreased by 1.
4	A	SO	C	BO	4	8	5	-5	0	5	4 contracts traded, 4 new contracts were created by the sell-to-open (SO). Both volume and open interest added 4.
5	C	SC	B	BO	3	11	5	-5	3	2	3 contracts were traded, but no new contracts were created or liquidated. Volume increased by 3, but the open interest stayed unchanged.
6	B	SC	A	BC	2	13	3	-3	1	2	2 contracts traded, 2 contracts were liquidated by buy-to-close (BC). Volume increased by 2, but open interest decreased by 2.
7	C	EX			1	13	2	-2	1	1	1 contract exercised (liquidated). Volume did not change but open interest reduced by 1.

In transaction #2, trader B sold-to-close (SC) 1 contract to trader C, who bought-to-open (BO). In this transaction, no new option contracts were created or liquidated. As a result, the volume added 1 contract, which now equals 3, while the open interest stayed at 2.

In transaction #3, trader B sold-to-close (SC) 1 contract to trader A, who bought-to-close (BC). In this transaction, one option contract was liquidated by the BC action. As a result, the volume added 1 contract, which now equals 4, while the open interest was reduced by one and now equals 1.

In transaction #4, trader A sold-to-open (SO) 4 contracts to trader C, who bought-to-open (BO). In this transaction, four new option contracts were created by the SO action. As a result, the volume added 4 contracts, which now equals 8, while the open interest added 4 contracts and now equals 5.

In transaction #5, trader C sold-to-close (SC) 3 contracts to trader B, who bought-to-open (BO). In this transaction, no new option contracts were added or liquidated. As a result, the volume added 3 contracts, which now equals 11, while the open interest stayed unchanged and remains at 5.

In transaction #6, trader B sold-to-close (SC) 2 contracts to trader A, who bought-to-close (BC). In this transaction, 2 option contracts were liquidated by the buy-to-close (BC) action. As a result, the volume added 2 contracts, which now equals 13, while the open interest dropped by two contracts and and now equals 3.

In transaction #7, trader C exercised 1 contract (action EX) and trader A was assigned 1 option. As a result, the volume has not changed, but the open interest dropped by one and equaled 2.

As the result of these seven transactions, the volume is 13 and open interest is 2. Trader A has 2 short (sold) positions, trader B has 1 long (holding) position, and trader C has 1 long (holding) position of the option. Note that the total number of contracts in the long positions of an option on the market should be equal to the total number of contracts in the short positions for the same option due to option parity, i.e. every option contract has two parties–a holding and a selling party.

As is evident from Table 4-1, each transaction, except for option exercise, increases volume. On the other hand, open interest may vary because some transactions create new options, some liquidate existing options, and some transactions neither create new nor remove existing options and, therefore, do not change the number of the existing options.

- ***Open interest*** of an option is the number of actually existing instances of option contacts at the moment.
- Options are created with "sell-to-open" and liquidated with "buy-to-close" or "exercise" transactions.

- Trading ***volume*** for options is the number of contracts of a given option that were traded during the period.
- Volume during one trading day is referred to as ***daily volume***.
- ***Option exercise*** does not change volume.

Self-Testing Questions and Exercises

Questions

7. What is an option contract?
8. How many minimum options can be traded?
9. What parameters are included in the option definition?
10. What does it mean to "write an option contract?"
11. What is the meaning of the terms trading "volume" and "open interest" for options?
12. What is the rationale for trading options?
13. What kind of trading shows a higher return on investment: stocks or options?

Exercises

6. Stock ABA is currently traded at a spot price of $38.00. What
7. A call with the strike price of $29.00 and the expiration date in two weeks is traded at $3.21 per call. The underlying stock is traded at $30.17 per share. What is the time value of the call?
8. You purchased two contracts of put options at $3.50 per option. How much did you pay for the transaction, excluding the commissions?
9. You purchased two contracts of "ABA June 19 2020 72 Put" at $4.20 per option and exercised it when the underlying stock price was $65.50. What was your profit and return on the

investment, excluding the commissions?

10. You purchased three contracts of "XYZ June19 2020 84.00 Call" at $5.50 per options and exercised it when the underlying stock price was $92.00. What was your profit and return on the investment, excluding the commissions.

5 Option Leverage and Greeks

5.1 Leverage Power of Options

Options offer a high leverage trading strategy. Suppose stock ABA is traded at $50 per share. The trader expects the stock price to go up.

Example 8

Scenario 1: The trader bought 100 shares of ABA for $50 per share, paid $50*100 = $5,000, held the shares for a month until the stock price reached $55 per share. The stock was sold for $55 per share with return on investment ROA = (55-50)/50 = 10% excluding commissions.

If the stock price falls to $48 the loss is (48-50)/50 = - 4% with a potential to recover if the stock position is not liquidated.

Scenario 2: The trader bought 1 contract of the ABA Call with the expiration in one month and strike price $50 for $2 per option. Excluding commissions, the trader paid $2*100 = $200. A month later, when the stock price was $55 per share, the trader exercised the option and bought 100 shares of ABA at the strike price of $50 per share. Immediately after exercising the option, the trader sold the shares at a market price of $55. As a result, the trader's return on investment is ROA = (55-50-2)/2 = 150%.

On the other hand, if the stock price fell to $48, instead of rising, then the loss is (0-2)/2 = - 100% without any chance to recover because the option became worthless upon expiration.

Thus, options allow for high leverage and high return on investment on one hand, but could cause high percentage losses if they fail.

In this and other examples with options, trading and exercise commissions are ignored for simplicity

5.2 Option Exercise vs. Option Trading

American options can be exercised at a strike price on or before the expiration date. If the option is not "in-the-money," the investor can just ignore it. Options become worthless after their expiration.

Options can also be traded. The total market value of an option varies depending on demand and supply, but never goes below the option intrinsic value. The option value (premium, market price) consists of two components, the option intrinsic value and the option time (extrinsic) value as shown in Eq.(3.3).

Thus, investors may purchase options with the intention to resell them when their market price is right to make profit.

Suppose one has purchased options, calls or puts. If the options are exercised, the holder receives their intrinsic value. However, if the options are sold then the holder receives the total market value of the options, which includes the intrinsic and extrinsic values. Taking into account that the extrinsic value (time value) of American options is always positive before the expiration and falls to zero at the expiration, it is more profitable to consider selling options than to exercise them if, for any reason, the trader wants to close a long option position before the expiration. At the option's expiration, the time value of options becomes zero, but it could be too late to sell the options, therefore, it is better to exercise options at their expiration, as though they were in-the-money. Sometimes, due to the spread between ask and bid, option exercise may be considered before the expiration.

5.3 Option Greeks

Option traders are interested to know how an option market price (premium) will react to changes to the underlying stock's price, how this reaction will vary over time as option expiration approaches, and what the chances are to be at-the-money, in-the-money, and out-of-the-money at the option expiration.

Complex theories and many parameters-indicators have been developed to provide answers to these questions. Historically, those parameters have been denoted with the letters of the Greek alphabet and, for this reason, the variety of the parameters used to assess options behavior are referred to as options Greeks.

The most frequently used is the Black-Sholes model for option pricing[8], which was originally developed to describe European options, but later extended to American options. The Cox, Ross, and Rubinstein discrete time binomial model[9] for American options was developed to simplify the description of the random process of option pricing with possible exercise at any moment before or on the expiration date.

5.3.1 Historical vs. Implied Volatility

Volatility, in general, is a parameter that shows possible fluctuation of prices, which is measured as standard deviation.

An option value (premium or price) consists of two components, intrinsic and extrinsic values. The intrinsic value represents the virtual profit that the investor can generate if he exercises the option right away and liquidates the new stock position on the open market. The extrinsic value or the time value of the option represents gain opportunities provided by the option in the future before the expiration. Imagine for a moment that the price of the underlying stock will never change, at least till the option expiration. In this case, the extrinsic value of the option is zero because the option intrinsic value is known and there is no opportunity in the future to gain more from the option. On the other hand, in the real world, stock prices do change. The higher the volatility of the underlying stock means there are more opportunities the option could offer in the future. The extrinsic value of options of such an underlying stock should be higher because of the potential for gain.

Historical volatility is the annualized actual standard deviation of the stock price measured for the certain period of time in the past. Investors may use this parameter to assess investment opportunities associated with the stock.

---

[8] Fischer Black and Myron Scholes (1973). The Pricing of Options and Corporate Liabilities, *The Journal of Political Economy*, Vol. 81, No. 3, pp. 637-654.

[9] John C. Cox, Stephen Ross, and Mark Rubinstein (1979). Option Pricing: A Simplified Approach, *Journal of Financial Economics*, vol. 7, No.3, p. 229. doi:10.1016/0304-405X(79)90015-1

Implied volatility is a parameter that represents the expected volatility of the underlying stock over the time before the option expiration.

It is impossible to predict, with certainty, an option's future value on or before the expiration; however, it would be quite desirable to be on the statistically expected side of possible changes according to the implied volatility. If implied volatility increases, then the related option market value goes up due to increased opportunities.

However, it would be wrong to believe that an option value depends only on implied volatility. An option value is affected by the following parameters:
- Current underlying price
- Options strike price
- Time until expiration, expressed as a percent of a year
- Implied volatility
- Risk-free interest rates

and implied volatility is just one of them. Thus, a more comprehensive analysis should be conducted to assess the potential of investing in options.

5.3.2 Delta

An option value depends on the price of the underlying stock. However, it may happen that the underlying stock moves in the expected direction, but the option doesn't. Sometimes options with different strike prices move contrary to the underlying stock's price. The answer to this puzzle is the market. The intrinsic value of an option and its underlying stock price are strongly correlated. The option time value depends on many parameters, but mostly depends on the time till expiration. The option market price (premium) also follows a random process obeying the odds of market demand and supply. To help investors understand and assess the market's odds and better navigate the options, a parameter is needed to describe the correlation of the option price changes to the underlying stock's price changes.

Delta (δ) is the parameter that shows how much an option price (premium) is theoretically expected to change if the price of the underlying stock changes by one dollar. The term "theoretically" implies an option pricing model. As a ratio, delta (δ) is defined as

5 Option Leverage and Greeks

$$\delta = \frac{\Delta V}{\Delta P} \quad \text{or} \quad \delta = \frac{dV}{dP} \tag{5.1}$$

where V is the market price (premium) of an option and P is the price of the underlying stock.

It is unreasonable to expect that the option value (market price, premium) could change in the future more than the expected price change of the underlying stock and, hence, one can conclude that its delta is positive and varies between zero and one for calls and is negative and varies between minus one and zero for puts, i.e.

$$\begin{array}{ll} \text{for Calls} : & 0 \leq \delta \leq 1 \\ \text{for Puts} : & -1 \leq \delta \leq 0 \end{array} \tag{5.2}$$

It should be noted that in-the-money options will react stronger on the stock price changes than out-of-the-money options. Also, options with a shorter time to expiration would react stronger on the stock price changes than the options with the longer time to expiration.

Suppose the premium for a Call is $2.40 and delta = 0.6. If the price of the underlying stock goes up by $0.75 then the expected change of the Call price is Δ Call Price = delta * Δ Stock Price = 0.6 * $0.75 = $0.45. Thus the new Call price is expected to be $2.40 + $0.75 = $3.15.

5.3.3 Gamma

Gamma (γ) is the rate at which delta changes when the underlying stock price changes by one dollar. Thus, delta can be interpreted as the speed that an option price can change relative to its underlying stock's price change. Therefore, gamma can be interpreted as the acceleration of that option price change. In the terms of ratio, gamma (γ) is

$$\gamma = \frac{\Delta \delta}{\Delta P} \quad \text{or} \quad \gamma = \frac{d\delta}{dP} = \frac{d^2\delta}{dP^2} \tag{5.3}$$

where V is the price of an option and P is the price of the underlying stock.

Example 9

Suppose there is a call option with strike price of $60 for ABA stock. The sample values of delta and gamma for different times till expiration are shown in Table 5-1. As is evident from the table, delta decreases as the expiration approaches.

Table 5-1: Illustration of delta and gamma (all data in US dollars)

		Stock price	$58	$59	$60	$61	$62
60 days to expiration	Delta		.31	.40	.50	.60	.79
	Gamma			.09	.10	.10	.09
1 day to expiration	Delta		.01	.11	.50	.89	.99
	Gamma			.10	.39	.39	.10

5.3.4 Vega

Vega (v) is the amount the option price can be expected to change for one-point change in implied volatility. Parameter vega affects only the time value of the option (extrinsic value) and does not have any effect on the intrinsic value of the option. In terms of ratio, vega (v) is

$$v = \frac{\Delta V}{\Delta \sigma} \quad \text{or} \quad v = \frac{dV}{d\sigma} \qquad (5.4)$$

where σ is the underlying stock's volatility.

Example 10

Suppose an option price is $2.00 and vega equals .06; this means that if the underlying stock volatility goes up by 1%, the option price will go up by .06 reaching $2.06 per option.

5.3.5 Theta

Theta (θ) measures how much will the time value of an option decline per one day as it approaches its expiration date, if all else remains unchanged.

$$\theta = \frac{\Delta V}{\Delta \tau} \quad \text{or} \quad \theta = \frac{dV}{d\tau} \qquad (5.5)$$

5 Option Leverage and Greeks

where τ is the time left till expiration. Parameter theta (θ) is measures in amount of money per day

Example 11

Suppose an option price is $8.72 and $\theta = 0.6$; this means that on the next trading day the option price is expected to drop by $8.72*.02 \approx$ $.17 to $8.55 per option, if there are no changes to the underlying stock's price.

5.3.6 Rho

Rho (ρ) is the amount an option price will change for one percent change in interest rate.

$$\rho = \frac{\Delta V}{\Delta r} \quad \text{or} \quad \rho = \frac{dV}{dr} \qquad (5.6)$$

Parameter rho (ρ) can be ignored for short-term options, but, for long term options, it may play an important role because changes in interest rates change the cost of carry.

Cost of carry is the cost incurred by holding an investment position. In financial analysis, it is always assumed that the money needed to open a position or for any other transaction is borrowed and, hence, interest should be paid to maintain this position as long as it is open. In general, the forward price can be calculated as

$$F = S\exp\bigl((r+s-c)\tau\bigr) \qquad (5.7)$$

where S is the spot price and F is the forward price, r is the risk-free interest rate, s is the storage cost rate, and c is the convenience yield, τ is the time difference between when the position was opened and closed, ($\tau = t_c - t_o$), t_c is time when the position was closed or expired and t_o is time when the position was opened. Thus, the cost of carry, CC, can be calculated as the difference between the forward and spot prices as

$$CC = S\bigl(\exp((r+s-c)\tau)-1\bigr) \qquad (5.8)$$

The storage cost can be applied to physical objects including commodities, but definitely does not apply to options. Options do not pay dividends, so convenience yield is not applicable to options.

Thus, the cost of carry for options consists of the risk-free interest only, i.e.

$$CC = S(\exp(r\tau) - 1) \tag{5.9}$$

5.3.7 Combination of Greeks

The former described parameters work better combined.

Example 12

Suppose the market price of an option is $V = \$6.84$, $\delta = .6$, and $\theta = .02$. What would be the expected price of the option on the next day ($\Delta\tau = -1$), if the price of the underlying stock goes up by $2.54 ($\Delta P = \$2.54$)? To answer this question, a combination of the impacts of delta and theta has to be applied. The option price is expected to change by $\Delta V = \Delta P^* \delta + \Delta\tau^*\theta = 2.54^*.06 - 1^*-02 = 1.52 - .02 = \$1.50$.

5.3.8 Summary of Greeks

Table 5-2 summarizes the options Greeks discussed above. The actual option assessment with the Greeks depends on the model used, but their meaning and interpretation stays.

Table 5-2: Summary of the Option Greeks

Black-Scholes Factor	Greek	Mathematical Expression	
		Discrete	Derivative
Stock price, P	Delta, δ	$\delta = \dfrac{\Delta V}{\Delta P}$	$\delta = \dfrac{dV}{dP}$
	Gamma, γ	$\gamma = \dfrac{\Delta\delta}{\Delta P}$	$\gamma = \dfrac{d\delta}{dP} = \dfrac{d^2\delta}{dP^2}$
Volatility (sigma, σ)	Vega, υ	$\upsilon = \dfrac{\Delta V}{\Delta\sigma}$	$\upsilon = \dfrac{dV}{d\sigma}$
Time till expiration, (tau, τ)	Theta, θ	$\theta = \dfrac{\Delta V}{\Delta\tau}$	$\theta = \dfrac{dV}{d\tau}$
Risk-free interest rate, r	Rho, ρ	$\rho = \dfrac{\Delta V}{\Delta r}$	$\rho = \dfrac{dV}{dr}$

5.4 Options Offer Great Opportunities but be Careful with Them

Options offer excellent high leverage investment opportunities. However, every coin has two sides. The inexperienced investors may put too much cash in options and just hope for good luck with the underlying stock. However, if luck is lacking, things may go differently and the investor may face significant losses, as the options expire out-of-the money. This is the reason why options are considered a high risk investment and are not recommended for beginners. On the other hand, with proper knowledge and experience, investing in options can offer high potential investment opportunities.

Self-Testing Questions and Exercises

Questions

1. What kind of trading shows a higher return on investment: stocks or options?
2. Why is option trading riskier than stocks?
3. What is understood by the term "option Greeks?"
4. What is the difference between historical and implied volatilities?
5. Why is implied volatility needed in options trading?
6. What is the definition of the parameter "delta," what does it mean, and why is it needed?
7. What is the definition of the parameter "gamma," what does it mean, and why is it needed?
8. What is the definition of the parameter "vega," what does it mean, and why is it needed?
9. What is the definition of the parameter "theta," what does it mean, and why is it needed?
10. What is the definition of the parameter "rho," what does it mean, and why is it needed?
11. What is "cost of carry" and why is it needed?

Exercises

1. The value of an option is $6.24, its delta is 0.5, and the price

for the underlying stock is $82.00. What will be the expected price of the option if the price for the underlying stock drops to $80.50?

2. The value of an option is $3.16, its vega is 0.7. What will be the expected price of the option if the volatility of the underlying stock increases by $0.8?

3. The value of an option is $5.64, its theta is 0.06. What will be the expected price of the option on the following day if the price of the underlying stock does not change?

6 Long Options

6.1 Operations and Hedging with Options

Options offer high return and protective strategies by providing the right to buy the underlying stock at the strike price with calls and the right to sell the underlying stock at the strike price with puts that serve as insurance to investors. Such protection allows investors to use options for hedging their portfolios. On the other hand, high trading leverage may put options in a highly aggressive category of investment. The level of risk assumption an investor is able and willing to assume depends on their investment goals and the strategies. For this reason, options are considered a highly risky investment and are not recommended for beginners.

By buying calls or puts, the holder acquires the right to exercise an option under favorable circumstances before or at the expiration, or may simply ignore it. By selling short, or synonymously, **writing** a call, the seller, in exchange for the premium received from the option buyer, accepts the obligation to sell the underlying stock to the option buyer at the strike price in the future before or on the expiration date if the option buyer (holder) decides to exercise the option. Similarly, by selling short, or synonymously, **writing** a put, the seller, in exchange for the premium received from the option buyer, accepts the obligation to buy the underlying stock from the option buyer (holder) at the strike price, if the option buyer (holder) decides to exercise the option before or on the expiration date. When an option is exercised by the option holder, the option seller, who holds the short position of the option, must fulfill the obligation to the option holder. The fulfillment of the obligation, from the option seller's side, is referred to as **option assignment**.

American options can be exercised on any trading day before or on the day of expiration. Exercising American options before expiration normally makes very little sense because of positive time value of American options. Typically, it is more profitable for the option holder to close a long option position by selling the options rather than to exercise them if the transaction is performed before the option expiration. By exercising an option before expiration, the option holder gets its intrinsic value, while, by selling the same options to close the long option position, the holder gets the option market price, which is the sum of the intrinsic and the time value of the option. The time value of an American option is always positive due to the opportunities associated with the option. Such an opportunity diminishes over time and turns into zero at its expiration.

Every option is normally traded in much smaller volumes than the underlying stock. One of the reasons for this is a vast variety of options, calls and puts, with different strike prices and expiration dates available for each stock. Due to relatively low trading volumes for each option type, sometimes it is hard or even impossible to sell an option due to a high spread (ask-bid) or just simply the absence of a reasonable bid. Due to this fact, time-to-time American options are exercised before the expiration, but it is an exception caused by limited trading volumes rather than by the nature of options.

It is worth mentioning that European options allow theoretical negative time value due to their exercising limitations. However, we are not discussing trading strategies with European options in this book.

The major component of an option value is its intrinsic value, which depends on the option strike price and the spot price of the underlying stock, as was presented in Eq.(10.2) in the previous chapter.

Options are mostly traded for profit, as any other securities, as their market prices change. Typically, listed options change hands many times before their expiration.

The analysis of options is conducted in this book for American options only. Thus, the options in this book are assumed American options unless specially noted.

6 Long Options

> - *All options* in this book are assumed to be *American options* unless otherwise noted.
> - *All trading commissions are ignored* in the gain/loss analysis for the sake of simplicity. The commissions can be easily included in the analysis by the reader if needed.

> Options can be either
> - *traded for profit* as their market price change similarly to other securities or
> - *exercised* if their intrinsic value is positive

> Options are normally exercised on or near the expiration day, when their time value is low or nears zero.

For the sake of simplicity, we will ignore transaction commissions because commissions are typically negligible compare to trading amounts. It is quite easy to add commissions to an analysis, if needed.

> When an option is exercised by the option holder, the option seller, who holds the short option position, has to fulfill their obligation of selling in the case of a call or buy; in the case of a put, the appropriate number of shares of the underlying stock is sold to the option holder at the strike price. The fulfillment of the obligation from the seller's side is referred to as *option assignment*.

6.2 Long Calls and Puts

The term *long options*, consequently, long calls or long puts, refers to the options bought and held by an investor for the purpose of selling them for profit in the future, similar to the long positions of stocks. Long calls and puts are the most natural uses of options.

6.3 Closing Long Calls and Puts by Selling Them

As was mentioned above, options can be traded for profit as any other security. The gain from trading options, calls or puts, is calculated similarly to trading other securities as

$$G = D - C \qquad (6.1)$$

where G is the gain, C is the premium (value) per option, at which the option position was open (bought for long options), D is the value of the option at which the option position was closed (sold, exercised, or expired). A negative gain implies a loss.

There are three major differences between trading long options and trading stocks:

- an investor can hold long positions of stocks as long as practical, but options expire and, hence, cannot be held beyond expiration because they become worthless.
- if the stock price does not change over time, the intrinsic value of any option associated with that stock will stay unchanged, too; however, the option will keep losing its value over time due to the option time value decay.
- option time value depends on the time remaining until expiration and on the difference between the strike price and the underlying stock price. For this reason, the option time value may temporarily increase over time; however, it will fall to zero at expiration.

Eq.(6.1) can be rewritten in term of the option intrinsic and extrinsic (time) values at the times of buying and selling the option as

$$G = V_{Intr}^{Close} + V_{Time}^{Close} - V_{Intr}^{0} - V_{Time}^{0} = \Delta V_{Intr} + \Delta V_{Time} \qquad (6.2)$$

where V_{Intr}^{0} and V_{Intr}^{Close} are the intrinsic values of the option at the time of open and close the option position, V_{Time}^{0} and V_{Time}^{Close} are the time values of the option at the time of open and close the position, and

$$\Delta V_{Intr} = V_{Intr}^{Close} - V_{Intr}^{0} \quad \text{and} \quad \Delta V_{Time} = V_{Time}^{Close} - V_{Time}^{0} \qquad (6.3)$$

Intrinsic value of an option V_{Intr} is defined as following:

$$\begin{aligned}\text{for a Call} &: V_{Intr} = \max(P-K, 0)\\ \text{for a Put} &: V_{Intr} = \max(K-P, 0)\end{aligned} \qquad (6.4)$$

where K is the option strike price and P is the price of the underlying stock.

If a long option position is closed by selling the options, then the gain/loss is calculated similarly to the same operation with stocks, as the difference between the sale and buy prices.

6.4 Exercising Long Calls or Puts

Long calls and puts, can be exercised by the option holder if the intrinsic value of the options is positive, otherwise exercising the option makes no sense. Please note that long options, with positive intrinsic values, which are not approaching their expiration, better be sold rather than exercised because of the additional profit resulting from positive time values of options before their expiration.

Gain/Loss Assessment

For the gain/loss assessment of exercised options, the stock position opened in the option exercise is assumed to be immediately closed at a market price. If it was a call, then, in the option exercise, the underlying stock is bought at a strike price and assumed to be immediately sold at the market price. If it was a put, then, the short position of the underlying stock is opened by selling the stock at a strike price and assumed to be immediately closed by buying to cover the stock at the market price.

The transactions involved in the calculation of the gain from the exercised option are shown in Figure 6-1.

It is not required to close the long option position by exercising the option; however, these possibly virtual transactions are used for the gain/loss assessment. Thus, the gain from an exercised option is calculated as the difference of the option intrinsic value at the time of the option exercise, V_{Intr}^{Close}, and the option purchase price (premium) C as

$$G = D - C = V_{Intr}^{Close} - V_{Intr}^{0} - V_{Time}^{0} \qquad (6.5)$$

where V_{Intr}^0 and V_{Time}^0 are the intrinsic and the time value of the option at the moment the option is purchased. Please note that the time value of the option at the time of exercise is not included in Eq.(6.5) because the option holder receives only the option intrinsic value at option exercise.

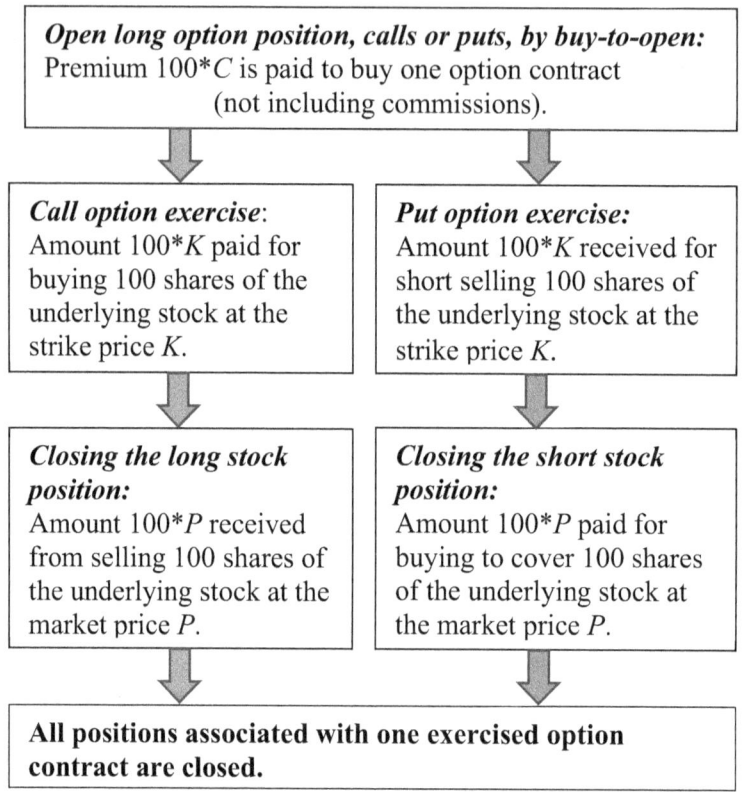

Figure 6-1: Standard transactions for the gain assessment in exercising options. The transactions of the left side represent call options and, on the right side, put options

The dependence of the gain from an option exercise on the price of the underlying stock at the time of the option exercise is shown in Figure 6-2(a) for a call and Figure 6-2(b) for a put.

The intrinsic value of the option, a call and a put, is shown in Figure 6-2 by a dotted line and the total gain from the investment, closed by option exercise, is shown by the solid line in the same figure.

The investment in a long call, closed by the option exercise, results in a gain (a positive gain) if the price of the underlying stock exceeds $K+C$ at the exercise time, where K is the strike price and C is the call purchased price. If the price of the underlying stock falls below $K+C$ at the exercise time, then the investment results in a loss (negative gain) with the maximum loss of C, i.e. the amount paid for the call. Thus, a potential gain from a long call position is unlimited while the maximum possible loss is limited to the amount paid for buying the call.

The investment in a long put, closed by the option exercise, results in a gain if the price of the underlying stock declines below $K-C$ at the exercise time. If the price of the underlying stock exceeds $K-C$ at the put exercise time, then the investment results in a loss (negative gain) with the maximum loss of C, i.e. the amount paid for the put. Thus, a potential gain from a long put position is limited to $K-C$, i.e. the put strike price less the put buy price, while the maximum possible loss is limited to the amount initially paid for the put to open a long put position.

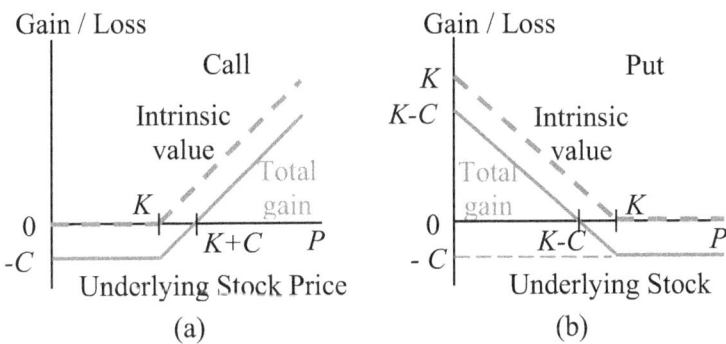

Figure 6-2: The gain/loss from an option exercise (a) for a call and (b) for a put as a function of the underlying stock price. K is the option strike price, C is the premium paid for the option, P is the price of the underlying stock at the time of option exercise. The option intrinsic value is shown with the dashed line and the total gain with the solid red line.

> The ***potential gain from a long call position*** is unlimited, while the ***maximum possible loss*** is limited to the amount paid for buying the call.

> The ***potential gain from a long put position*** is limited to K-D, the strike price less the put buy price, while the ***maximum possible loss*** is limited to the amount initially paid for the put to open a long put position.

6.5 Strategy with Long Options

Long options provide good leverage and are very helpful in increasing the return on investment and reducing risk when traders are not sure about the direction of the stock's price trend. However, the premium paid for buying options can be completely lost if the intrinsic price of option does not reach the level necessary to end with a gain. Please note that having a positive intrinsic value of the option is not enough because, according to Eq.(6.2) and Figure 6-2, the intrinsic value should exceed the option purchase price to secure a gain. Also, investing in options may consume all available cash and lead to an unrecoverable loss of cash in the case of an option failure.

Example 1: A Long Call at the Expiration

One contract of calls "ABA June 12 2020 15 Call" with the strike price $K = \$15$ was purchased at price (premium) $C = \$2.40$ per call when the ABA stock was traded at $P_0 = \$16.25$ per share. Thus, the initial intrinsic value of the call was $V_{Intr}^0 = P_0 - K = \$16.25 - \$15.00 = \$1.25$ and the time value was $V_{Time}^0 = C - V_{Intr}^0 = \$2.40 - \$1.25 = \$1.15$. At the expiration, the price of ABA stock was $P = \$18.70$. Then at the expiration, the intrinsic value of the call was $V_{Intr}^E = P - K = \$18.70 - \$15.00 = \$3.70$. The gain from this call was $G = V_{Intr}^0 - C = \$3.70 - \$2.40 = \$1.30$. The total gain from one contract "ABA June 12 2020 Call" is $G*100 = \$130.00$ because each contract consists of 100 options.

6 Long Options

Example 2: A Long Put at the Expiration

Two contracts "XYZ August 21, 2020 20 Put" with the strike price $K = \$20.00$ was purchased at price (premium) $C = \$2.20$ per put when the XYZ stock was traded at $P_0 = \$20.75$ per share. Thus, the put was out-of-the-money and its intrinsic value was zero, i.e. $V^0_{Intr} = 0$. The time value of the put was $V^0_{Time} = C - V^0_{Intr} = \$2.20$. At the expiration, the price of the XYZ stock was $P = \$15.42$. Then the intrinsic value of the put was $V^{Close}_{Intr} = K-P = \$20.00-\$15.42 = \$4.58$ and the time value $V^{Close}_{Time} = 0$. The total gain from these two contracts is $200* G = 200*(V^0_{Intr} - C) = 200*(\$4.58-\$2.20) = \$476.00$.

Self-Testing Questions and Exercises

Questions

1. Which is more profitable: to sell (sell-to-close) or exercise a long option before expiration?
2. Would a long option, which expired "in-the-money", be automatically exercised?
3. Can a long option, expired "in-the-money", result in a loss for its holder?
4. What is the highest potential gain/loss for a long call?
5. What is the highest potential gain/loss for a long put?

Exercises

In the following exercises, please ignore price spread (ask minus bid) and transaction commissions, unless some special condition is specified in the exercise.

1. One contract of ABA calls with the strike price of $25 was purchased at $3.00 per call. Later, the contract was sold for $4.50 per call. What was the gain or loss from this transaction?
2. One contract of XYZ calls with the strike price of $30 was purchased at $8.00 per call at a time when the underlying stock was traded at $35.00 per share. The stock was traded at $32.00 at the call's expiration. What was the gain or loss of the holder of this call contract?

3. Two contracts of ABA puts with the strike price of $45.00 were purchased at $3.50 per put at a time when the underlying stock was traded at $46.00 per share. The stock was traded at $41.00 at the put's expiration. What was the gain or loss of the holder of these put contracts?

4. Two contracts of ABA puts with the strike price of $45.00 were purchased at $11.00 per put at a time when the underlying stock was traded at $42.00 per share. The stock was traded at $48.00 at the put's expiration. What was the gain or loss of the holder of these put contracts?

7 Short Options

7.1 The Sense of Short Options

If an investor sells-to-open options, calls or puts, the investor **writes the option sells options short**, or opens a **short option position**. All the above terms are synonyms of the same action that results in a short option position, which can be referred to as a **short call** or a **short put,** subject to the option type. With a short call position, the investor takes the obligation to sell to the option buyer (holder) one share of the underlying stock at the strike price per each call option if the call gets assigned, i.e. if the call is exercised before or at the expiration. With the short put position, the investor takes the obligation to buy from the option buyer (holder) one share of the underlying stock at the strike price per each put option if assigned, i.e. if the put is exercised by the put buyer before or at its expiration. Please remember that options are traded or exercised by contracts only, one hundred options per each contract.

The term "*short*" is used for option positions created by writing options (sell-to open) by analogy with short stock positions, though the mechanism of short stock and short option positions are fundamentally different. By opening a short stock position, the trader borrows the appropriate quantity of shares of the stock from the brokerage and sells it in the market, taking the obligation to buy and return the borrowed shares (not money) to the broker in the future. By opening a short option position (sell-to open), the trader creates a new instance of the option and takes the obligation to sell (for a call) or to buy (for a put) the appropriate number of shares of the underlying stock to the holder of the option, if the option holder decides to exercise the option. Thus, the terms "*short*" have different meaning for the stocks and options. Both, short positions of stocks or options are shown with the negative number of shares(for stocks) and contracts (for options) in the trader's account.

Thus, the term "***selling an option short***" means writing the option, which is fundamentally different from the term selling the stock short.

A short call, alone, not being hedged with a long position of the underlying stock or other options of the same underlying stock in the portfolio to secure the potential sale of the underlying stock if the call is exercised by the option buyer, is referred to as a ***naked call***. Similarly, a short put, not being hedged with a short position of the underlying stock or other options of the same underlying stock in the portfolio to secure the potential purchase of the underlying stock if the put is exercised by the option buyer, is referred to as a ***naked put***. The term **write a call** or **write a put** refers to selling options short (sell-to-open), calls or puts, to open a short option position. This action is equivalent to creating new instances of the options, which adds one unit to the count of the open interest to the option per each option contract sold short (sell-to-open).

Short option positions can be closed by
- buying the option to close (buy-to-close),
- assigning the option if the option holder exercises it, or
- expiration when the option becomes worthless.

With any of the above actions, the option ceases to exist and the count of the open interest decreases by one unit per each closed option contact.

The first action to close a short option position, buy-to-close, is similar to closing a short stock position and results in a gain or loss according to Eq.(6.1).

The gain from naked calls and puts, at expiration or assignment, is shown in Figure 7-1 as a function of price P of the underlying stock at the time of expiration or assignment.

The gain, G, from the naked options, at any time, if assigned or expired, is equal to the initial amount received from selling the option short (sell-to-open), C, less the intrinsic value of the option at assignment or expiration, V_{Intr}^{Close}, shown with the solid red line in Figure 7-1.

Eq.(7.1) implies that the time value of an option is discarded at assignment (option exercise by the holder) or is reduced to zero at expiration. The gain in Eq.(7.1) is derived from Eq.(6.1) because the option seller is liable to the option holder for the intrinsic value of the option at assignment. The intrinsic value at its expiration is zero. Thus, one can conclude that the option seller is liable to the option holder for the intrinsic value of the option at the expiration.

$$G = C - V_{Intr}^{Close} \qquad (7.1)$$

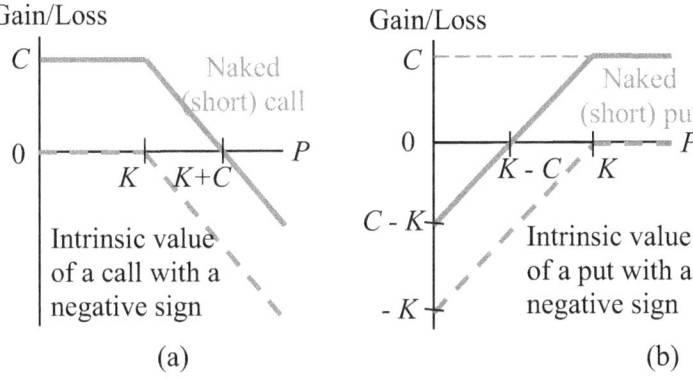

Figure 7-1: Gain/loss for naked options at any time, when assigned or expired: (a) for a naked call and (b) for a naked put as a function of the underlying stock price; K is the option strike price, C is the premium received from initially selling the option to open, P is the price of the underlying stock at the option assignment or expiration. The intrinsic value of the option with the negative sign is shown with the dotted line and the total gain with the solid red line.

The initial amount, C, received from the option buyer, for writing the option, is equal to the value of the option at the time of the short sale, which is equal to the sum of the intrinsic and time values of the option at the time of the option short sale (sell-to-close), i.e.

$$C = V_{Intr}^{0} + V_{Time}^{0} \qquad (7.2)$$

where V_{Intr}^{0} is the option initial intrinsic value and V_{Time}^{0} is the option time value at the time of selling the option short (sell-to-open). Thus, the gain can be expressed as the difference between the intrinsic value of the option at the time of writing the option (selling it short), V^0_{Intr}, and at the assignment or expiration, V^{Close}_{Intr}, plus the time value of the option at the time of writing the option, V^0_{Time},

$$G = V^0_{Intr} - V^{Close}_{Intr} - V^0_{Time} \qquad (7.3)$$

The initial amount C received by the option seller from the option buyer is the essence of the strategy with naked calls and puts. This amount is received at the time of the option short sale. Assume, the intrinsic value of the option at selling it short (writing the option) equals the intrinsic value at the time of assignment or expiration, i.e. $V^{Close}_{Intr} = V^0_{Intr}$, then the gain from the naked option is equal to the option time value at the time selling it short, V^0_{Time}, i.e.

$$G = V^0_{Time} \quad \text{if} \quad V^{Close}_{Intr} = V^0_{Intr} \qquad (7.4)$$

This is an advantage of short (naked) options versus the short sale of a stock.

The amount C constitutes the maximum possible gain from the naked option, which is the essence of the strategy with naked options. If the option expires at-the-money, i.e. $P = K$, then the naked option ends up with the gain equal C. Naked options will result in a loss if the price of the underlying stock exceeds $K+C$ for the naked call or declines below $K-C$ for the naked put.

- A **short call** not being hedged with a long position of the underlying stock or other options of the same underlying stock in the portfolio to secure the potential sale of the underlying stock if the call is exercised by the option buyer, is referred to as a **naked call**.
- A **short put** not being hedged with a short position of the underlying stock or other options of the same underlying stock in the portfolio to secure the potential purchase of the underlying stock if the put is exercised by the option buyer, is referred to as a **naked put**

7 Short Options

> The essence of *short options* is in time decay of the extrinsic (time) value of options.

The rational of long options is that the trader buys the option and expects the option to get deeper in-the-money to sell or to exercise it. The rational of short options is quite opposite. The trader writes an option and immediately receives the money for it with the expectation that the option will expire out-of-the-money releasing the option writer from the obligation due to the option exercise by the holder.

The essence of short options is in time decay. By writing an option, the trader receives the premium equal the full value of the option, including its time value, but at the time of expiration, the time value drops to zero. Thus, even if the price of the underlying stock stays unchanged, the option writer gains due to the time value decay. The greater underlying stock volatility, the higher the option time value, and the better investment opportunities may come from writing options.

Self-Testing Questions and Exercises

Questions

1. What does it mean "writing an option"?
2. What are short options?
3. What are naked calls and puts?
4. What is the difference between a naked call and a short call?
5. What is the difference between a naked put and a short put?
6. What is the difference between writing an option and selling the option short?
7. How is an option short sale different from a stock short sale?
8. What is the rationale for writing options (selling options short)?

Exercises

In the following exercises, please ignore price spread (ask minus bid) and transaction commissions, unless some special condition is specified in the exercise.

1. A call with the strike price of $37.00 was written at $3.00 per

call when the underlying stock was traded at $38.00 per share. What was the time value of the call at that time?

2. A put with the strike price $42.00 was sold short at $6.50 at the time when the underlying stock was traded at $42.00. What was the time value of the put at the expiration?

3. A call with the strike price of $50.00 was written for $4.00 when the underlying stock's price was $48.00 per share. Draw the gain/loss chart for the naked call at expiration.

4. Stock ABA is currently traded at the spot price of $38.00 and a put with the strike price of $38.00 was sold short at $3.00. The price of the underlying stock was 38.00, the same as at the time of selling put short. Has the put writer (short seller) gained or lost at the transaction?

5. A put with the strike price of $40.00 was sold short at $4.20 when the price of the underlying stock was $38.00 per share. Draw the gain/loss chart for the naked put.

6. One contract of calls with the strike price $82.00 was written at $8.00 at the time when the underlying stock was traded at $81.00. The underlying stock, at the option expiration, was traded for $80.00. What is the gain or loss from this call at expiration?

8 Naked Calls

8.1 Naked (Short) Calls

A short call, alone, not being hedged with a long position of the underlying stock or other options of the same underlying stock in the portfolio to secure the potential sale of the underlying stock if the call is exercised by the option buyer, is referred to as a ***naked call***..

The gain/loss chart of a naked call (a short call), as a function of the underlying stock's price at assignment or expiration is shown in Figure 7-1(a), where the intrinsic value of the call, with the negative sign, is shown with a dashed line, while the solid line represents the total gain/loss.

Amount C received from short selling a call is the gain, if the call has expired out-of-the money. This strategy will yield a gain, even if the call has ended in-the-money with the intrinsic value not exceeding C. It means that if the price of the underlying stock, at its expiration, exceeds the strike price K by an amount less than C, the naked call will still be profitable as it is evident from Figure 7-1(a). Thus, amount C, received from short selling the call (sell-to-open), is a potential gain, which serves as a cushion for the option seller if the underlying stock price goes in the wrong direction, i.e. grows above the strike price K but not above $K+C$.

However, if the underlying stock price grows above $K+C$, the loss from the naked call is potentially unlimited. The value of C equals the sum of intrinsic value V_{Intr}^{0} and time value V_{Time}^{0} of the call at the time of the option short sale as in Eq.(7.2). The initial intrinsic value of the call V_{Intr}^0 depends on the call strike price K and the underlying stock price P_0 at the time of writing the naked call[10],

$$\text{short call: } V_{Intr}^0 = \max(P_0 - K, 0) = \begin{cases} P_0 - K & \text{for } K < P_0 & \text{in-the-money} \\ 0 & \text{for } K = P_0 & \text{at-the-money} \\ 0 & \text{for } K > P_0 & \text{out-of-the-money} \end{cases} \quad (8.1)$$

As is evident from Eq.(7.5), the initial intrinsic value of a call at-the money and out-of-the-money is zero. For this reason, here and elsewhere on this book when assessing the gain/loss for options we may ignore the "at-the-money" status because it implies a zero intrinsic value, which matches the values of both, "in-the-money" and "out-of-the-money," at the price of the underlying security equal to the option strike price. Thus, the amount C received from selling short a call with the strike price K at the time when the underlying stock price was P_0 is

$$C = V_{Intr}^0 + V_{Time}^0 = \\ = \begin{cases} P_0 - K + V_{Time}^0 & \text{for } K < P_0 & \text{(in-the-money)} \\ V_{Time}^0 & \text{for } K \geq P & \text{(out-of-the-money)} \end{cases} \quad (8.2)$$

The intrinsic value of the call at the assignment or expiration, V_{Intr}^{Close}, is

$$V_{Intr}^{Close} = \max(P - K, 0) = \\ = \begin{cases} 0 & \text{for } P \leq K & \text{(out-of-the-money)} \\ P - K & \text{for } P > K & \text{(in-the-money)} \end{cases} \quad (8.3)$$

where P is the price of the underlying stock at its expiration. Note that the time value of an option is equal to zero at assignment (option exercise by the holder) or expiration. Then, according to Eq.(7.1), the total gain, G, from the naked call, at the assignment or expiration, equals the initial cash received from selling the call short (sell-to-open), C, less the intrinsic value of the call at the assignment or the expiration, V_{Intr}^{Close}, i.e.

---

[10] Synonymous terms like "writing the naked call," "selling the call short," and "selling call to open" and similar terms are used interchangeably to familiarize the reader with these terms.

8 Naked Calls

For a short call:
$$G = C - V_{Intr}^{Close} = \min(C, C+K-P) =$$
$$= \begin{cases} C & \text{for } P \leq K \text{ (out-of-the-money)} \\ C+K-P & \text{for } P > K \text{ (in-the-money)} \end{cases} \quad (8.4)$$

A Naked Call with the Strike Price Lower than the Stock Price at the Time of Sale ($K < P_0$)

If a call is sold short (sell-to-open), with the strike price K lower than the spot price of the underlying stock P_0 at the time of sale, i.e. $K < P_0$, then the value of C is high because the call is in-the-money and its premium equals the intrinsic value of the call $P_0 - K$ and the time value of the call according to Eq.(7.6) as

$$C = V_{Intr}^0 + V_{Time}^0 = P_0 - K + V_{Time}^0 \quad (8.5)$$

The **breakeven price,** $P_{BE,}$ of the naked call is the price of the underlying stock at which the naked call ends up with a zero gain if assigned or expired, i.e.

$$P_{BE} = K + C = K + V_{Intr}^0 + V_{Time}^0 = K + P_0 - K + V_{Time}^0 = P_0 + V_{Time}^0 \quad (8.6)$$

The breakeven point for the naked call, with the strike price lower than the underlying stock price at the time of writing the call, is illustrated in Figure 8-1(a). The call is in-the-money at that time and, hence, its intrinsic value is high and equal to $P_0 - K$.

The maximum possible gain from a naked call, with $K < P_0$, is high enough because of the high initial intrinsic value of the call. However, the risk associated with the naked call is quite high, too, because the naked call will result in a loss if the underlying stock price rises by ΔP_{BE},

$$\Delta P_{BE} = P_{BE} - P_0 = P_0 + V_{Time}^0 - P_0 = V_{Time}^0 \quad (8.7)$$

and exceeds the breakeven price P_{BE}.

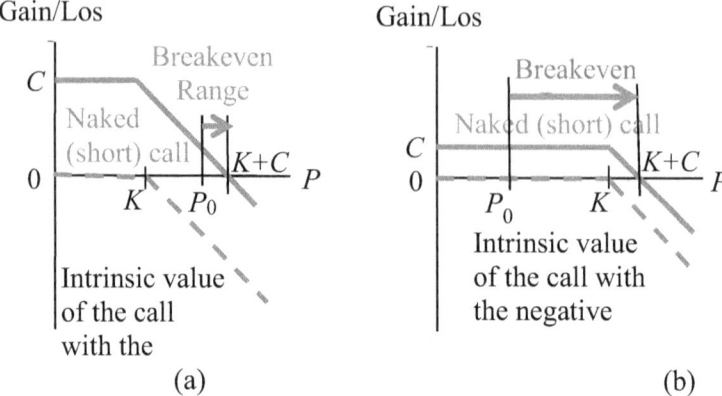

Figure 8-1: Gain/loss for a naked call: (a) for the strike price K lower than the underlying stock price P_0 at the time of the call sell, $K < P_0$, and (b) for the strike price higher (or equal) than the underlying stock price at the time of the call sell, $K \geq P_0$

The price difference between the initial price of the underlying stock at the time of writing the call (the short sale of the call), ΔP_{BE}, is referred to as the **breakeven range**. The breakeven range provides a safety cushion for possible price variations of the underlying stock to keep the naked option positive at its expiration. The cushion is quite narrow in this case and equals the time value of the call at the time of writing the call. The breakeven range, in terms of the percentage change of the underlying stock price, can be expressed as

$$\frac{\Delta P_{BE}}{P_0} = \frac{V^0_{Time}}{P_0} \qquad (8.8)$$

According to Eqs.(7.6) and (7.8), gain G from the naked (short) call with $K < P_0$ can be calculated as

$$\text{short call: } K < P_0 : G = \begin{cases} C = P_0 - K + V^0_{Time} & \text{for } P < K \\ C + K - P = P_0 - P + V^0_{Time} & \text{for } P \geq K \end{cases} \qquad 8.9)$$

where P_0 is the price of the underlying stock at the time of selling the call short and P is the price of the stock at the time of assignment

8 Naked Calls

or expiration. The maximum possible gain G_{Max} of a naked call with $K < P_0$ is quite high because the call was in-the-money at the time of selling it short,

$$G_{Max} = C = V_{Intr}^0 + V_{Time}^0 = P_0 - K + V_{Time}^0 \qquad (8.10)$$

For the naked call to end up with the maximum gain C at the expiration the underlying stock should drop at least by

$$\Delta P_{Max} = P_0 - K \qquad (8.11)$$

to decline below K. In terms of a percentage rate, the required stock price drop to receive the maximum possible gain is

$$\frac{\Delta P_{Max}}{P_0} = \frac{P_0 - K}{P_0} = 1 - \frac{K}{P_0} \qquad (8.12)$$

A Naked Call with the Strike Price Greater than the Stock Price at the Time of Sale ($K \geq P_0$)

If a call is sold short (sell-to-open) with the strike price, K, greater than the spot price of the underlying stock, P_0, at the time of writing the call, i.e. $K \geq P_0$ then the value of C is equal to the call time value, V_{Time}^0, only because the initial intrinsic value of the call equals zero according to Eq.(7.5). The gain/loss chart for $K \geq P_0$ is shown in Figure 8-1(b).

The **breakeven price** P_{BE} of a naked call with $K \geq P_0$ can be calculated as

$$P_{BE} = K + C = K + V_{Intr}^0 + V_{Time}^0 = K + V_{Time}^0 \qquad (8.13)$$

because the intrinsic value of the call, at the time of its writing, was zero according to Eq. (7.5). In this case, the risk associated with the naked call is quite low due to a wide breakeven range $\Delta P_{BE,}$ which is

$$\Delta P_{BE} = K + C - P_0 = V_{Time}^0 + K - P_0 \qquad (8.14)$$

that exceeds the time value of the call at the time of the short sale by the difference between the call strike price and the price of the underlying stock at the time of the call sale as illustrated in Figure 8-1(b). The breakeven range, expressed as a percentage change of the underlying stock price change, is

$$\frac{\Delta P_{Max}}{P_0} = \frac{V_{Time}^0 + K - P_0}{P_0} = \frac{V_{Time}^0}{P_0} + \frac{K - P_0}{P_0} \qquad (8.15)$$

According to Eq.(7.6), gain G from the naked (short) call with $K \geq P_0$ can be calculated as

$$\text{short call: } K \geq P_0 : G = \begin{cases} C = V_{Time}^0 & \text{for } P < K \\ C + K - P = K - P + V_{Time}^0 & \text{for } P \geq K \end{cases} \qquad (8.16)$$

where P_0 is the price of the underlying stock at the time of writing the call (sell-to-open) and P is the price of the stock at the time of assignment or expiration. The maximum possible gain G_{Max} of a naked call with $K \geq P_0$ is relatively low because the call was out-of-the-money or at-the-money at the time it was sold short,

$$G_{Max} = C = V_{Time}^0 \qquad (8.17)$$

For the naked call with $K \geq P_0$ to end up with the maximum gain, C, at assignment or expiration, the underlying stock price P could vary widely and may rise up to the strike price K, keeping the naked call in maximum gain $G_{Max} = V_{Time}^0$. This range for the underlying stock to grow, ΔP_{Max}, is

$$\Delta P_{Max} = K - P_0 \qquad (8.18)$$

In terms of a percentage rate, the required stock price drop to receive the maximum possible gain is

$$\frac{\Delta P_{Max}}{P_0} = \frac{P_0 - K}{P_0} = 1 - \frac{K}{P_0} \qquad (8.19)$$

The call has a good chance to stay and expire out-of-the-money because $K \geq P_0$. The gain from the naked call, in this case, is limited to the time value of the call at the time of writing the call, V_{Intr}^0, but provides an extensive price cushion $\Delta P_{BE,}$ calculated in

8 Naked Calls

Eq.(7.17) for the variations of the underlying stock price to stay profitable at expiration.

The Breakeven Stock Price with a Naked Call

The **breakeven price** is the price of the underlying stock at assignment or expiration of a naked option at which the total gain from the naked option equals zero. The breakeven price for a naked call can be expressed according to Eqs.(7.10) and (7.17) as

$$P_{BE} = K + C = K + V^0_{Intr} + V^0_{Time} = \begin{cases} P_0 + V^0_{Time} & \text{for } K < P_0 \\ K + V^0_{Time} & \text{for } K \geq P_0 \end{cases} \quad (8.20)$$

Please note that the breakeven price for a naked call, P_{BE}, is always greater than the price of the underlying stock at the time of the option sale, P_0, i.e.

$$P_{BE} > P_0 \quad (8.21)$$

The breakeven range, ΔP_{BE}, is a price cushion for the underlying stock to keep the naked call profitable. According to Eqs.(7.10) and (7.17), the breakeven range is

$$\Delta P_{BE} = K + C - P_0 = K + V^0_{Intr} + V^0_{Time} - P_0 = \begin{cases} V^0_{Time} & \text{for } K < P_0 \\ V^0_{Time} + K - P_0 & \text{for } K \geq P_0 \end{cases} \quad (8.22)$$

and

$$\frac{\Delta P_{BE}}{P_0} = \begin{cases} \dfrac{V^0_{Time}}{P_0} & \text{for } K < P_0 \\ \dfrac{V^0_{Time} + K - P_0}{P_0} & \text{for } K \geq P_0 \end{cases} \quad (8.23)$$

The breakeven range for a naked call is quite narrow with $K < P_0$ and gets wider with $K \geq P_0$. Taking into account that the initial time value of the option, V^0_{Time}, declines with the distance between the strike price K and the stock price at the time of selling the call, P_0, as shown in Figure 3-4, the price cushion, ΔP_{BE}, becomes greater with the lower strike price K.

> - The **breakeven price** is the price of the underlying stock at which the short option ends up at assignment or expiration without gain or loss.
> - The **breakeven range** is the range between the breakeven price and the price of the underlying stock at which the short option was sold.

8.2 Gain/Loss with a Naked Call

The gain with the naked call at assignment or expiration, G, can be expressed according to Eq.(7.8) as

$$\text{short call: } G = \begin{cases} C & \text{for } P < K \quad \text{(out-of-the-money)} \\ C + K - P & \text{for } P \geq K \quad \text{(in-the-money)} \end{cases} \quad (8.24)$$

where P is the price of the underlying stock at the call assignment or expiration. The maximum possible gain G_{Max} can be expressed according to Eqs.(7.14) and (7.21) as

$$G_{Max} = \begin{cases} P_0 - K + V^0_{Time} & \text{for } K < P_0 \\ V^0_{Time} & \text{for } K \geq P_0 \end{cases} \quad (8.25)$$

Example 3: A Naked Call with $K < P_0$

One contract of a call of ABA stock with the strike price of $K = \$210.00$ and expiration in 3 months was sold short (sell-to-open) at $C = \$47.00$, when the stock price was $P_0 = \$250.00$ per share. The call was initially in-the-money. The intrinsic (Eq.(7.5)) and the time (Eq.(7.2)) values of the call at the time of short sale (sell-to-open) were

$$\begin{aligned} V^0_{Intr} &= P_0 - K = \$250.00 - \$210.00 = \$40.00; \\ V^0_{Time} &= C - V^0_{Intr} = \$47.00 - \$40.00 = \$7.00 \end{aligned} \quad (8.26)$$

The breakeven price (Eq.(7.24)) and the breakeven range (Eq.(7..26)) for the naked call were

8 Naked Calls

$$P_{BE} = K + C = \$210.00 + \$47.00 = \$257.00;$$
$$\Delta P_{BE} = P_{BE} - P_0 = \$257.00 - \$250.00 = \$7.00; \quad (8.27)$$
$$\frac{\Delta P_{BE}}{P_0} = \frac{\$7.00}{\$250.00} = 3\%$$

The underlying stock price at the expiration is $P = \$246.00$, which is greater than the call strike price. Then, taking into account that $P > K$, the gain from the naked call at expiration G can be calculated with Eq.(7.28) as

$$G = K + C - P = \$210 + \$47.00 - \$246.00 = \$11.00 \quad (8.28)$$

As is evident from Eq.(7.32), the naked call ended up at expiration with a gain regardless that the underlying stock price exceeded the call strike price. It occurred because of the cushion provided by the breakeven range.

Options are traded by contracts. As it was 1 contract of the naked calls, that means 100 calls, then the total gain was $11.00*100 = $1,100 per contract.

Example 4: A Naked Call with $K > P_0$

Two contracts of a call of XYZ stock with the strike price of $K = \$210.00$ and expiration in 3 months was sold to open at $C = \$7.00$ when the stock price was $P_0 = \$170.00$ per share, so the call was out-of-the-money. The intrinsic (Eq.(7.5)) and the time (Eq.(7.2)) values of the call at the time of short sale (sell-to-open) were

$$V_{Intr}^0 = \$0 \quad \text{and} \quad V_{Time}^0 = C - V_{Intr}^0 = \$7.00 \quad (8.29)$$

The breakeven price P_{BE} (Eq.(7.24)) and the breakeven range ΔP_{BE} (Eq.(7.26)) for the naked call were

$$P_{BE} = K + C = \$210.00 + \$7.00 = \$217.00;$$
$$\Delta P_{BE} = P_{BE} - P_0 = \$217.00 - \$170.00 = \$47.00; \quad (8.30)$$
$$\frac{\Delta P_{BE}}{P_0} = \frac{\$47.00}{\$170.00} = 28\%$$

In this case, the possible maximum gain was only $7.00 per call, but the safety cushion provided by the breakeven range ΔP_{BE} was quite wide, equal to $47.00.

Suppose the underlying stock price had risen by $45.00 and reached at the expiration $P = \$215.00$, which was greater than the strike price K, thus, the call expired in-the-money with the intrinsic value

$$V_{Intr} = P - K = \$215.00 - \$210.00 = \$5.00 \quad (8.31)$$

As the call was expiring in-the-money, it was assigned to the call seller. Despite this, the naked call ended up with a gain for the call seller. The gain was

$$200 * G = 200 * (C - V_{Intr}) = 200 * (\$7.00 - \$5.00) = \$400.00 \quad (8.32)$$

per call. The gain of the naked call with the call expired in-the-money shown in Eq.(7.36) became possible due to the wide cushion ΔP_{BE} calculated in Eq.(7.34).

The comparison of the breakeven ranges in this and the previous examples clearly show that the relative breakeven range in this example, $\Delta P_{BE}/P_0 = 28\%$, is much greater than that in the previous example, $\Delta P_{BE}/P_0 = 3\%$. The chances that the underlying stock price would move more than 28% are much lower than the chances that the price would move by 3%, like in the previous example. This provides a much better price cushion for the naked call in this example.

As the transaction was for 2 call contracts, the total gain was $2.00*200 = \$400$ for 2 contracts.

8.3 Strategies with Naked Calls

Naked calls could be considered if the underlying stock is expected to fall, similar to short selling the stock. However, naked calls offer a much higher rate of return and offer a price range cushion for the underlying stock, which is referred to as the breakeven range, ΔP_{BE}.

The higher the strike price, the greater is the maximum possible gain, G_{Max}, but the price cushion, ΔP_{BE}, becomes narrower.

Naked calls with the strike price, K, greater than the stock price at the time of writing the call (sell-to-open), P_0, i.e. $K > P_0$, are safer due to a wider breakeven range ΔP_{BE}, though they offer a

8 Naked Calls

lower maximum possible gain, G_{Max} is equal to the initial time value of the call, V_{Time}^0. On the other hand, naked calls with the strike price, K, lower than the stock price at the time writing the call (sell-to-open), P_0, i.e. $K < P_0$, offers a higher maximum possible gain, G_{Max}, but is exposed to a much higher risk due to a narrower breakeven range.

Self-Testing Questions and Exercises

Questions

1. What is a naked call?
2. What is the difference between a naked call and a short call?
3. What is the difference between writing a call and selling the call short?
4. How is a call short sale different from a stock short sale?
5. What is the rationale for naked calls?
6. How would a naked call expire (with profit or with loss) if the price of the underlying stock at the expiration equals the price of the stock at the time of writing the call?
7. What is the highest potential gain/loss for a naked call?
8. What is a breakeven price of the underlying security for a short call?
9. What is a breakeven range for the underlying security for a short call?
10. What is the relationship between the strike price K and the price of the underlying stock at the time of writing a call P_0 at which the breakeven range ΔP_{BE} is wider?
11. How does the breakeven range relate to the gain from the short options?

Exercises

In the following exercises, please ignore price spread (ask minus bid) and transaction commissions, unless some special condition is specified in the exercise.

1. A call with the strike price of $42.00 was written at $7.00 per call when the underlying stock was traded at $45.00 per share. What was the time value of the call at that time?

2. A call with the strike price of $50.00 was written for $4.00 when the underlying stock's price was $48.00 per share. Draw the gain/loss chart for the naked call at expiration.
3. Stock ABA is currently traded at the spot price of $38.00 and a call was written at-the-money for $3.00. Draw the gain/loss chart for the naked put at expiration.
4. A call with the strike price of $40.00 was sold short at $4.20 when the price of the underlying stock was $38.00 per share. Calculate the breakeven price and the breakeven range of the underlying stock. Draw the gain/loss chart for the naked put.
5. One contract of calls with the strike price $90.00 was written at $8.00 at the time when the underlying stock was traded at $89.00. The stock, at the call expiration, was traded for $95.00. What is the gain or loss from this call at the expiration?

9 Naked Puts

9.1 Naked (Short) Puts

A short put, not being hedged with a short position of the underlying stock or other options of the same underlying stock in the portfolio to secure the potential purchase of the underlying stock if the put is exercised by the option buyer, is referred to as a ***naked put***.

A gain/loss chart for a naked put (a short put) is shown in Figure 7-1(b) as a function of the underlying stock price. The intrinsic value of the put with a negative sign is shown in the figure with a dashed line, while the total gain is shown with a solid line. The total gain includes the amount received for selling the put short and paid in the put assignment. If the put expires out-of-the-money or in-the-money, then the put seller receives no assignment. Similar to the naked call, the initial amount, C, received from selling a put short (sell-to-open) represents a maximum possible gain if the put expires out-of-the-money or at-the-money. The naked put will not lose money even if the price of the underlying stock falls below the put strike price down to $K - C$.

If the underlying stock price falls below $K - C$ the loss from the naked put could go up to $C - K$ as it is shown in Figure 7-1(b). In contrast to a naked call, the maximum potential loss with a naked put is limited.

The value of C, the amount received from selling the put short, is the sum of the put intrinsic value and the time value as shown in Eq.(7.2). The intrinsic value of a put, V_{Intr}^0, at the time of sell the put short (sell-to-open) is

$$\text{put: } V_{Intr}^0 = \max(0, K - P_0) = \begin{cases} 0 & \text{for } K \leq P_0 \quad \text{(out-of-the-money)} \\ K - P_0 & \text{for } K > P_0 \quad \text{(in-the-money)} \end{cases} \quad (9.1)$$

where P is the price of the underlying stock at the put assignment or expiration and K is the put strike price.

According to Eq.(7.1) the total gain, G, from the naked put if assigned or expired equals the initial cash received from selling the put short (sell-to-open), C, less the intrinsic value of the put at the assignment or the expiration, V_{Intr}^{Close}, i.e.

$$\text{short put: } G = C - V_{Intr}^{Close} = \min(C, C + P - K) = \\ = \begin{cases} C + P - K & \text{for } P < K \quad \text{(in-the-money)} \\ C & \text{for } P \geq K \quad \text{(out-of-the-money)} \end{cases} \quad (9.2)$$

where P is the price of the underlying stock at the put assignment or expiration and K is the put strike price and the intrinsic value of the put at that time V_{Intr}^{Close} is

$$\text{put: } V_{Intr}^{Close} = \max(K - P, 0) = \begin{cases} 0 & \text{for } P \geq K \quad \text{(out-of-the-money)} \\ K - P & \text{for } P < K \quad \text{(in-the-money)} \end{cases} \quad (9.3)$$

A Naked Put with the Strike Price Lower than the Stock Price at the Time of Sale ($K < P_0$)

If a put is sold short (sell-to-open) with the strike price K lower than the spot price of the underlying stock P_0, i.e. $K \leq P_0$, then the initial intrinsic value of the put V_{Intr}^0 dropped to zero according to Eq.(7.37) and, hence, the value of C is equal to the time value of the put at the time of the short sale of the put, V_{Time}^0. In this case, the put is out-of-the-money at the time of writing the put and the **breakeven price** P_{BE} of the naked put if assigned or expired is illustrated in Figure 9-1(a) and equal to

$$P_{BE} = K - C = K - V_{Time}^0 \quad (9.4)$$

9 Naked Puts

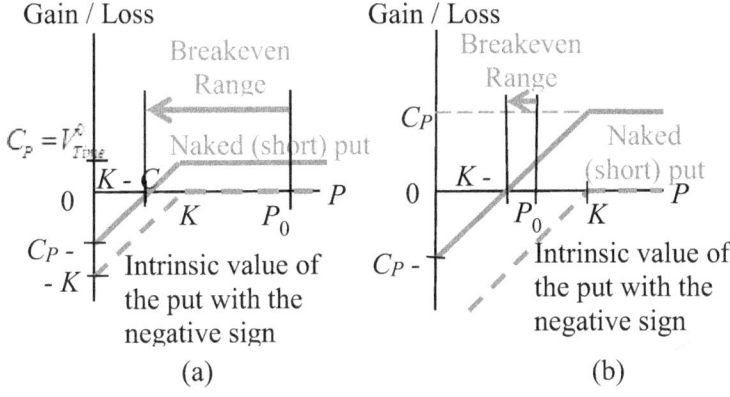

Figure 9-1: Gain/loss for a naked put: (a) for the strike price lower (or equal) than the underlying stock price at the time of the put short sell, $K \leq P_0$, and (b) for the strike price higher than the underlying stock price at the time of the put sell, $K > P_0$

The breakeven range of the put is quite wide

$$\Delta P_{BE} = P_0 - P_{BE} = P_0 - K + C = P_0 - K + V_{Time}^0 \quad (9.5)$$

and the relative breakeven range expressed in terms of percentage change of the underlying price is

$$\frac{\Delta P_{BE}}{P_0} = \frac{V_{Time}^0 + P_0 - K}{P_0} \quad (9.6)$$

that means that risk associated with this naked put is reasonably low because a relatively wide breakeven range as shown in Figure 9-1(a). The cushion provided by the breakeven range ΔP_{BE} is quite wide. According to Eq.(7.42), ΔP_{BE} is greater than the initial time value of the put, V_{Intr}^0. Thus, the lower the strike price K, the less risky the naked put is due to an increasing breakeven range, but the maximum possible gain G_{Max}

$$G_{Max} = C = V_{Time}^0 \quad (9.7)$$

declines too because according to Figure 3-4 in the previous chapter V_{Time}^0 declines with the growing difference between the strike price K and the price of the underlying stock at the time of the option short sale, P_0. According to Figure 3-4, the maximum time value of an option takes place when the strike price equals the spot stock price of the underlying stock.

Taking into account that C is composed of the initial time value and the initial intrinsic value as in Eq.(7.2), the initial intrinsic value of a put can be calculated as in Eq. (7.37), and according to Eq.(7.38), gain G from the naked (short) put with $K < P_0$ can be calculated as

$$\text{short put with } K < P_0 : \quad G = \begin{cases} P - K + C = V_{Time}^0 + P - K & \text{for } P < K \\ C = V_{Time}^0 & \text{for } P \geq K \end{cases} \quad (9.8)$$

A Naked Put with the Strike Price Greater than the Stock Price at the Time of Sale ($K \geq P_0$)

If a put is sold short with a strike price K greater than the spot price of the underlying stock P_0, i.e. $K \geq P_0$, then the value of C is relatively high because of a high initial intrinsic value of the put which according to Eq.(7.37) is equal to $K - P_0$. Risk associated with the naked put in this case is quite high, too, because the breakeven price is closer to the initial stock price, P_0, than in the previous case, i.e.

$$P_{BE} = K - C = K - V_{Time}^0 - V_{Intr}^0 = K - K + P_0 - V_{Intr}^0 = P_0 - V_{Time}^0 \quad (9.9)$$

and, hence, the breakeven range—the stock price cushion—is quite narrow and equal to the initial time value of the put, V_{Time}^0, only, i.e.

$$\Delta P_{BE} = P_0 - K + C = P_0 - K + V_{Intr}^0 + V_{Time}^0 = V_{Time}^0 \quad (9.10)$$

as illustrated in Figure 3-4(b). The percentage relative breakeven price is

$$\frac{\Delta P_{BE}}{P_0} = \frac{V_{Time}^0}{P_0} \quad (9.11)$$

9 Naked Puts

Thus with the naked put sold with the strike price greater than the spot price of the underlying stock, $K > P_0$, the possibility

$$\text{short put with } K \geq P_0 : \quad G = \begin{cases} C = K - P_0 + V_{Time}^0 & \text{for } P < K \\ P - K + C = P - P_0 + V_{Time}^0 & \text{for } P \geq K \end{cases} \quad (9.12)$$

and the maximum possible profit is

$$G_{Max} = C = V_{Intr}^0 + V_{Time}^0 = K - P_0 + V_{Time}^0 \quad (9.13)$$

A short put, with $K > P_0$, has a potentially high maximum gain with the higher risk of a loss due to a narrow low price cushion in the stock price trends in a wrong direction.

The Breakeven Stock Price with a Naked Put

The breakeven price for a naked put can be expressed as

$$P_{BE} = K - C = K - V_{Intr}^0 - V_{Time}^0 = \begin{cases} K - V_{Time}^0 & \text{for } K \leq P_0 \\ P_0 - V_{Time}^0 & \text{for } K > P_0 \end{cases} \quad (9.14)$$

Please note that the breakeven price for a naked put is always lower than the price of the underlying stock at the time of the option sale, i.e.

$$P_{BE} < P_0 \quad (9.15)$$

The breakeven range, ΔP_{BE}, that plays a role of a price cushion for the underlying stock to keep the naked put in profit according to Eqs.(7.41) and (7.46) is

$$\Delta P_{BE} = P_0 - P_{BE} = \begin{cases} V_{Time}^0 + P_0 - K & \text{for } K < P_0 \\ V_{Time}^0 & \text{for } K \geq P_0 \end{cases} \quad (9.16)$$

and

$$\frac{\Delta P_{BE}}{P_0} = \begin{cases} \dfrac{V_{Time}^0 + P_0 - K}{P_0} & \text{for } K < P_0 \\ \dfrac{V_{Time}^0}{P_0} & \text{for } K \geq P_0 \end{cases} \qquad (9.17)$$

The breakeven range for a naked put is quite wide with $K < P_0$ and narrows down to the initial time value of the put when $K \geq P_0$. Taking into account that the initial time value of the option V_{Time}^0 declines with the distance between the strike price K and the stock price at the time of selling the put short P_0 as shown in Figure 3-4, the price cushion, ΔP_{BE}, is greater with the lower strike price K.

> - The **breakeven price** is the price of the underlying stock at which the short option ends up at assignment or expiration without gain or loss.
> - The **breakeven range** is the range between the breakeven price and the price of the underlying stock at which the short option was sold.

9.2 Gain/Loss with a Naked Put

The gain with the naked put at assignment or expiration, G, can be calculated according to Eq.(7.38) as

$$G = \begin{cases} C + P - K & \text{for } P < K \\ C & \text{for } P \geq K \end{cases} \qquad (9.18)$$

where P is the price of the underlying stock at the put expiration and maximum possible gain G_{Max} is calculated as

$$G_{Max} = C = \begin{cases} V_{Time}^0 & \text{for } K \leq P_0 \\ K - P_0 + V_{Time}^0 & \text{for } K > P_0 \end{cases} \qquad (9.19)$$

9.3 Strategies with Naked Puts

Naked puts could be considered for investment if the underlying stock is expected to rise, similar to a long position of the stock. However, naked puts offer a limited gain, but a much higher

9 Naked Puts

rate of return with a price range cushion for the underlying stock, which is referred to as the breakeven range, ΔP_{BE}.

The higher the strike price, the greater is the maximum possible gain, G_{Max}, however, the price cushion, ΔP_{BE}, is narrower.

Naked puts with the strike price, K, lower than the stock price at the time of writing the put (sell-to-open), P_0, i.e. $K < P_0$ are safer due to a wider breakeven range ΔP_{BE} though they offer a lower maximum possible gain, G_{Max}, equal to the initial time value of the put, V_{Time}^0. On the other hand, naked puts with the strike price, K, greater than the stock price at the time writing the put (sell-to-open), P_0, i.e. $K > P_0$ offer a higher maximum possible gain, G_{Max}. but is exposed to a much higher risk due to a narrower breakeven range.

Example 5: A Naked Put with $K < P_0$

A put of ABD stock with the strike price of $K = \$210.00$ and expiration in 3 months was sold to open at $C = \$7.00$ when the stock price was $P_0 = \$250.00$ per share. Thus, the intrinsic value (Eq.(7.37)) and the time value (Eq.(7.2)) of the put at the time of sale were

$$V_{Intr}^0 = \$0 \quad \text{and} \quad V_{Time}^0 = C - V_{Intr}^0 = \$7.00 \qquad (9.20)$$

The breakeven price P_{BE} (Eq.(7.40)) and the breakeven range ΔP_{BE} (Eq.(7.41)) for the naked put are

$$\begin{aligned} P_{BE} &= K - C = \$210.00 - \$7.00 = \$203.00; \\ \Delta P_{BE} &= P_0 - P_{BE} = \$250.00 - \$203.00 = \$47.00; \\ \frac{\Delta P_{BE}}{P_0} &= \frac{\$47.00}{\$250.00} = 19\% \end{aligned} \qquad (9.21)$$

Suppose the underlying stock price at the assignment or expiration is $P = \$206.00$, which is below the put strike price, K, but above the breakeven price, $P_{BE} = \$203.00$. Taking into account that $P > K$ and $K < P_0$, the gain from the naked put at the assignment or expiration G can be calculated with Eq.(7.44) as

$$G = P - K + V_{Time}^0 = \$206.00 - \$210.00 + \$7.00 = \$3.00 \qquad (9.22)$$

Thus, the naked put safely ended up at assignment or expiration with the gain of $3.00 per a put, regardless that the underlying stock price declined from $P_0 = \$250$ at the time of the put sale to $P = \$206.00$ at the put assignment or expiration. This occurred because of a wide safety cushion provided by the naked put with the strike price chosen below the underlying stock price at the time of the put sale, i.e. $K < P_0$.

Options are traded by contracts. If it was 1 contract of the naked puts, that means 100 puts, then the total gain was $\$3.00*100 = \$300.00$ per contract.

It means that the stock declined by

$$\frac{P_0 - P}{P_0} = \frac{\$250.00 - \$206.00}{\$250.00} = 17.6\% \qquad (9.23)$$

but still kept the naked put in profit.

Thus, if $K < P_0$. The naked put does not offer a large gain but the chances for the gain are quite high even if the underlying stock significantly declines, but not below $K - C$.

Example 6: A Naked Put with $K > P_0$

A put of stock XYZ with the strike price of $K = \$210.00$ and expiration in 3 months was sold to open at $C = \$47.00$ when the stock price was $P_0 = \$170$ per share. Thus, the intrinsic value (Eq.(7.37)) and the time value (Eq.(7.2)) of the put at the time of sale were

$$\begin{aligned} V_{Intr}^0 &= K - P_0 = \$210.00 - \$170.00 = \$40; \\ V_{Time}^0 &= C - V_{Intr}^0 = \$47.00 - \$40.00 = \$7.00 \end{aligned} \qquad (9.24)$$

The breakeven price (Eq.(7.45)) and the breakeven range (Eq.(7.46)) for the naked put are

$$\begin{aligned} P_{BE} &= K - C = \$210.00 - \$47.00 = \$163.00; \\ \Delta P_{BE} &= P_0 - P_{BE} = \$170.00 - \$163.00 = \$7.00; \\ \frac{\Delta P_{BE}}{P_0} &= \frac{\$7.00}{\$170.00} = 4\% \end{aligned} \qquad (9.25)$$

The possible maximum gain from the naked put in this case is quite high, $C = \$47.00$ per put, if the underlying stock price rises to or above the strike price $K = \$210.00$ at the expiration. However, the breakeven range ΔP_{BE} in this case is quite narrow and equals

9 Naked Puts

$7.00—only this makes the case potentially lucrative, but quite risky compared to the case in the previous example.

If the underlying stock price at the assignment or expiration rises above $210.00 per share, the naked put ends up with maximum gain of

$$G_{Max} = C = \$47.00 \tag{9.26}$$

per put.

If the underlying stock price at the assignment or expiration falls to $P = \$165.00$, i.e. the stock price trends in the wrong direction. The naked put still yields a profit of

$$G = P - K + C = \$165.00 - \$210.00 + \$47.00 = \$2.00 \tag{9.27}$$

per put. However, if the underlying stock falls below $163.00 per share, the naked put ends up with a loss.

Thus, the naked put with $K \geq P_0$ offers a good gain, if the stock price trends in the right direction, however this put provides a very narrow protective cushion, ΔP_{BE}, and can easily turn into a loss.

Self-Testing Questions and Exercises

Questions

1. What are naked puts?
2. What is the difference between a naked put and a short put?
3. What is the difference between writing a put and selling the put short?
4. How is a put short sale different from a stock short sale?
5. What is the rationale for naked puts?
6. How would a naked put expire (with profit or with loss) if the price of the underlying stock at the expiration equals the price of the stock at the time of writing the put?
7. What is the highest potential gain/loss for a naked put?
8. What is a breakeven price of the underlying security for a short put?
9. What is a breakeven range for the underlying security for a short put?

10. What is the relationship between the strike price K and the price of the underlying stock at the time of writing a put P_0 at which the breakeven range ΔP_{BE} is wider?
11. How does the breakeven range relate to the gain from a short put?

Exercises

In the following exercises, please ignore price spread (ask minus bid) and transaction commissions, unless some special condition is specified in the exercise.

1. A put with the strike price of $45.00 was written at $7.00 per call when the underlying stock was traded at $43.00 per share. What was the time value of the put at that time?
2. A put with the strike price of $50.00 was written for $4.00 when the underlying stock's price was $51.00 per share. Draw the gain/loss chart for the naked call at expiration.
3. Stock ABA is currently traded at the spot price of $38.00 and a put with the strike price of $38.00 was sold short at $3.00. Calculate the breakeven price and the breakeven range for the naked put. Draw the gain/loss chart for the naked put at expiration.
4. A put with the strike price of $40.00 was sold short at $4.20 when the price of the underlying stock was $38.00 per share. Draw the gain/loss chart for the naked put.
5. One contract of puts with the strike price $90.00 was written at $8.00 at the time when the underlying stock was traded at $91.00. The stock, at its expiration, was traded for $86.00. What is the gain or loss from this put at expiration?
6. A put with the strike price $52.00 was sold short at $12.50 at the time when the underlying stock was traded at $45.00. What was the time value of the put at the expiration?

10 Trading Strategies with Single Options

10.1 Closing an Option Position by Trading vs Exercising the Option

A long option position can be closed either by selling it (sell-to-close) or by exercising it in-the-money (ITM), or by expiration out-of-the-money (OTM). A short option position can be closed either by buying-to-close or by expiring out-of-the-money (OTM), or by taking the assignment if the holder of the matching long option exercises it.

There are three ways to close an option position, either long or short. One way is to trade it, i.e. sell-to-close for a long option position or to buy-to-close for a short option position. Another way is to exercise a long option or to take an assignment for a short option, if the holder of the matching long option exercises it in-the-money (ITM). Also, if an option, long or short, expires out-of-the-money (OTM), the option position becomes worthless and is eliminated.

If an option expires ITM (in-the-money), the long option will be exercised and the matching short option will take an assignment. On the other hand, if an option expires OTM (out-of-the-money), the long option expires worthless. In this case, the holder of the long option ends up with a loss equal to the premium paid for the option and the short seller keeps the premium he received from writing (selling short) the option.

Let's note that an option status ATM (at-the-money) can be considered a border-line case of OTM, similarly with the zero intrinsic value. Therefore, we will not be analyzing this case separately from OTM.

10.1.1 Selling a Long Option vs Exercising

A holder of a long option position, call or put, has the right to exercise the option at any time before or at the expiration. Exercising the option, the holder receives the option's intrinsic value. Therefore, it makes sense to exercise long options, which are ITM (in-the-money). Taking into account that the option holder paid premium C to buy the option, the gain/loss for the option at the expiration or exercise is equal to the option intrinsic value received at the exercise less the premium paid for the option regardless whether the option was exercised before or at the expiration. If a long option expires OTM (out-of-the-money), the holder loses premium C paid for the option.

The solid line in Figure 10-3(a) for a long call and Figure 10-3(b) for a long put shows the intrinsic value of the option less the premium C paid for the option that represents the gain/loss for the appropriate long option at the exercise.

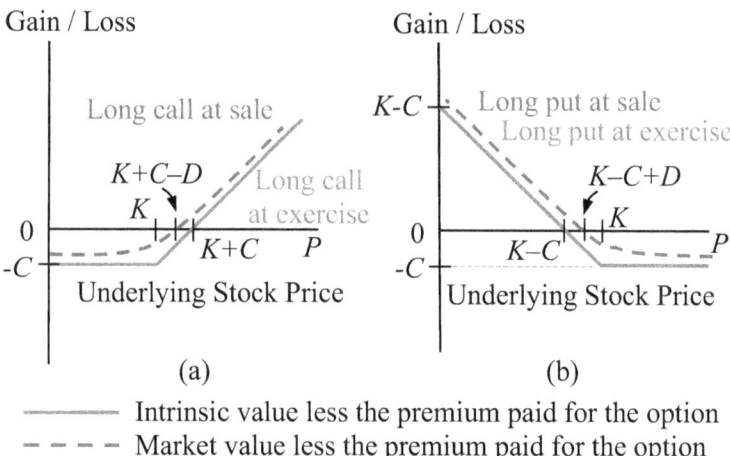

———— Intrinsic value less the premium paid for the option
- - - - Market value less the premium paid for the option

Figure 10-1: The gain/loss diagrams for a long (a) call and (b) put at exercise or expiration (the solid line) or when sold (the dashed curve) as a function of the underlying stock price P; K is the option strike price, C is the premium paid for buying the option, D is the premium received for selling the option

10 Trading Strategies with Single Options

Exercising a long call becomes profitable at the underlying stock price higher than $K+C$ (Figure 10-3(a)), where $K+C$ is the break-even point. Exercising a long put becomes profitable at the underlying stock price lower than $K-C$ (Figure 10-3,b), where $K-C$ is the break-even point.

If a long option position is closed by selling the option, then the seller receives premium D, which is the full value of the option equal the intrinsic value plus the time value of the option. The total gain/loss from selling the long option equals the premium received for selling the option, D, less the premium paid for the option, C.

The dashed curves in Figure 10-3 show the gain/loss diagram for a long option as a function of the spot price of the underlying stock at the time of selling the option. Figure 10-3(a) shows the gain/loss for selling a long call and Figure 10-3(b) for selling a long put.

The time value of an option depends on time till expiration as well as on the underlying stock price.

As we discussed in chapter 3, the time value of an option at any given time before the expiration is the highest at the price P of the underlying stock equal the option strike price K (Figure 3-2, Figure 3-3 and Figure 3-4).

As soon as the total value of an option is higher than its intrinsic value at any time before the expiration, it is generally better to sell a long option before the expiration than to exercise it, even if the option is ITM (in-the-money).

Selling a long call becomes profitable at the underlying stock price higher than $K+C-D$ (Figure 10-3,a), where $K+C-D$ is the break-even point. Selling a long put becomes profitable at the underlying stock price lower than $K-C+D$ (Figure 10-3,b), where $K-C+D$ is the break-even point.

Thus, the major goal of using long options is to exercise the options ITM at the expiration or to trade it for profit before the expiration. The trader first spends money to buy the options and later earns money by exercising or selling the options.

- The major goal of using long options is to exercise the options ITM at the expiration or to trade it for profit before the expiration.
- The trader first spends money to buy the options and later earns money by exercising or selling the options.

10.1.2 Buying-to-Close for a Short Option vs Taking Assignment

A short option position can be closed either by expiration OTM or by assignment if ITM, or by buying-to-close at any time before the option expiration.

If a short option position is closed by buying the option, then the option writer pays premium D, which is the full value of the option equal the intrinsic value plus the time value of the option. The total gain/loss from buying the option to close a short option position equals the premium C received for writing the option less the premium D paid later for the buying the option to close it. Taking into account the time value decay, the short option will be profitable even if the underlying stock price stays unchanged at the time of writing the option and closing the short option position (Figure 10-4).

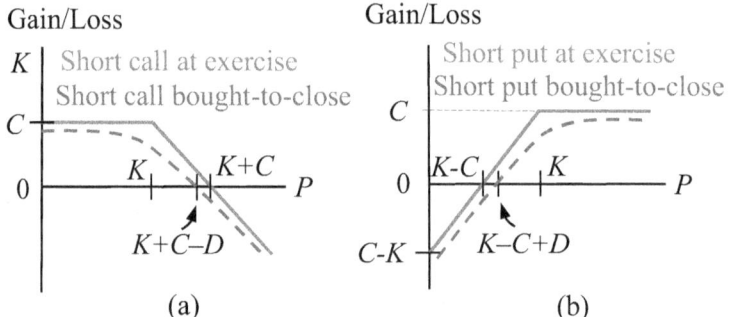

— Premium received for writing the option less the intrinsic value
- - - - Premium received for writing the option less the market value paid the option to close the position

Figure 10-2: The gain/loss diagrams for a short (a) call and (b) put at exercise or expiration (the solid line) or when bought-to-close (the dashed curve) as a function of the underlying stock price P; K is the option strike price, C is the premium received for writing (selling short) the option, D is the premium paid for buying the option to close the short option position

If expired or exercised by the long call holder, a short call becomes profitable at the underlying stock price lower than $K+C$ (Figure 10-4,a), where $K+C$ is the break-even point. It means that,

10 Trading Strategies with Single Options

if the underlying stock price is below K, the call is OTM and the holder of the matching long call would not exercise it. Thus, the call writer keeps the premium C received for writing the call. If the price of the underlying stock P is above K, the holder of the matching long call may exercise it that results in the assignment for the writer of the call. However, if the price for the underlying stock P is still below $K+C$, the premium received for writing the call is still higher than the assigned amount, thus keeping the short call profitable. Only when the price of the underlying stock P grows above $K+C$ the assigned amount exceeds the premium received for writing the call that results in the final loss.

A short put becomes profitable if expired or exercised by the long put holder at the underlying stock price P higher than $K-C$ (Figure 10-4,b), where $K-C$ is the break-even point. It means that, if the underlying stock price is above K, the put is OTM and the holder of the matching long put would not exercise it. Thus, the put writer keeps the premium C received for writing the put. If the price of the underlying stock P is below K, the holder of the matching long put may exercise it that results in the assignment for the writer of the put. However, if the price for the underlying stock P is still below $K-C$, the premium received for writing the put is still higher than the assigned amount, thus keeping the short put profitable. Only when the price of the underlying stock P falls below $K-C$ the assigned amount exceeds the premium received for writing the put that results in the final loss.

Thus, the major goal of writing options (short options) is to have them expire OTM or to trade it for profit before the expiration. The trader first collects money by writing an option and hopes the option to expire OTM not to get assignment or at least get the assignment for the lower amount than the amount collected for writing the option. Also, short options can be traded for profit or loss before expiration.

- The major goal of writing options (short options) is to have them expire OTM or to trade it for profit or loss before the expiration.
- The trader first collects money by writing an option and hopes the option to expire OTM not to get assignment or at least get the assignment for the lower amount than the amount collected for writing the option.

- Dealing with short options (writing the options) is the game of declining time value.
- The closer the strike price to the spot price of the underlying stock, the higher is the options time value.

10.2 Options vs Stock Positions

Options and stocks are different by their nature and, hence, by their trading strategies and by the associated risk. Both, stocks and options trading, have their own pros and cons and it is important to understand them and thoughtfully choose the situations, when to trade options and when to trade stocks.

In this section, we compare long and short option positions with the matching long and short positions of the underlying stock and analyze the advantages and disadvantages of trading options vs stocks, including potential gain and risk.

We ignore trading commissions for the sake of simplicity. Trading commissions are so low in the modern stock market that, we can easily ignore them in the analysis without compromising major conclusions.

The analysis conducted in this chapter compares one option with one share of the underlying stock. However, we all remember that options are traded in contracts only, one contract for one hundred options.

10.3 Long Options vs Stock Positions

By buying options (buy-to-open), the trader opens a long option position. It could be a long call or a long put position. In this section, we analyze long option positions vs the matching underlying stock positions.

10.3.1 A Long Call vs a Long Stock Position

Let's compare a long call with the strike price K purchased at premium C and a long position of the underlying stock opened at the stock price P_0. The gain/loss diagram of the long call is shown in Figure 10-3(a) and the gain/loss diagram of the long position of the underlying stock opened at stock price P_0 is shown in Figure 10-3(b).

10 Trading Strategies with Single Options

The solid line in Figure 10-3(a) shows the intrinsic value of the call less the premium C paid for the call that presents the gain/loss of the long call at expiration or exercise. The dashed curve in Figure 10-3(a) represents the gain/loss of the long call if sold before expiration. The difference between the dashed curve and the solid line in Figure 10-3(a) equals the time value of the call. As we have discussed in Chapter 3, the time value of an option at any given time before the expiration is the highest at the price P of the underlying stock equal the option strike price K (Figure 3-2, Figure 3-3 and Figure 3-4).

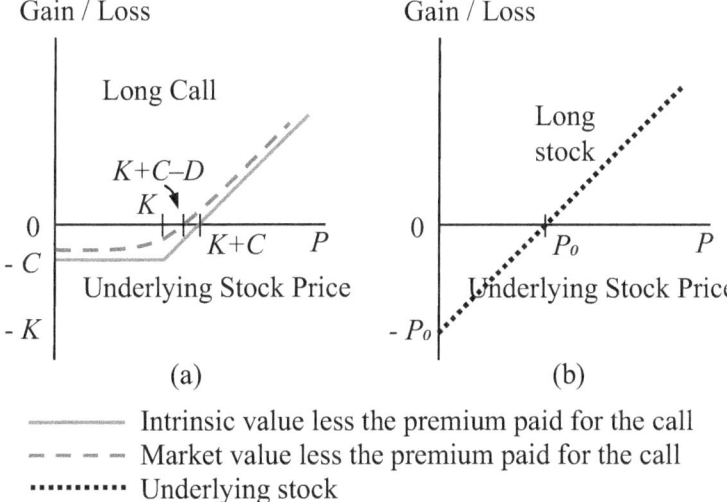

Figure 10-3: The gain/loss diagrams for (a) a long call at exercise or expiration (the solid line) or if sold at the market value (the dashed curve) and (b) a long position of the underlying stock as a function of the underlying stock price P; K is the call strike price, C is the premium paid for the call, P_0 is the underlying long stock purchase price, D is the premium received for selling the call

Both, a long call position and a long position of the underlying stock are targeting the expected uptrend of the underlying stock price. Both positions have unlimited maximum gain, if the underlying stock price keeps growing as shown in Figure 10-3(a). However, if the stock price drops below the stock purchase price P_0, the long stock position turns into a loss, with the maximum possible loss limited to the stock purchase price P_0 in case, if the stock price drops to zero as shown in Figure 10-3(b).

On the other hand, the maximum possible loss with the long call position is limited to the premium C paid for the call as the stock price falls below the call strike price (Figure 10-3(a)). Thus, the long call position offers a protection from the possible extended loss compare to the long position of the underlying stock in case when the underlying stock price falls.

Note, that the solid line in Figure 10-3(a) shows the gain/loss at exercise or expiration, while the dashed curve in Figure 10-3(a) shows the gain/loss, if the option is traded (sold) before the expiration.

10.3.2 A Long Put vs a Short Stock Position

Compare a long put with the strike price K purchased at premium C and a short position of the underlying stock opened at the stock price P_0. The gain/loss of the long put at exercise or expiration is equal to the intrinsic value of the put less the premium C paid for the put as shown in Figure 10-4(a) and the gain/loss diagram of the short position of the underlying stock opened at stock price P_0 is shown in Figure 10-4(b).

Both, a long put and a short stock positions are targeting the stock price to go down. The maximum possible gain with a short stock position is limited to the stock short sale price P_0, in case, if the stock price drops to zero as shown in Figure 10-4 (b). The maximum gain with the long put position is limited to $K - C$, which is the put strike price less the premium paid for the put (Figure 10-4 (a)).

However, if the underlying stock price rises above the short sale price P_0, the stock short position turns into a loss with the unlimited maximum loss, if the stock price keeps going up as shown in Figure 10-4(b). On the other hand, the maximum possible loss with the long put position is limited to C, the premium paid for the put as the stock price rises above the put strike price (Figure 10-4(a)). Thus, the long put position offers a good protection from the possible extended loss compared to the short position of the underlying stock, if the underlying stock price shows uptrend.

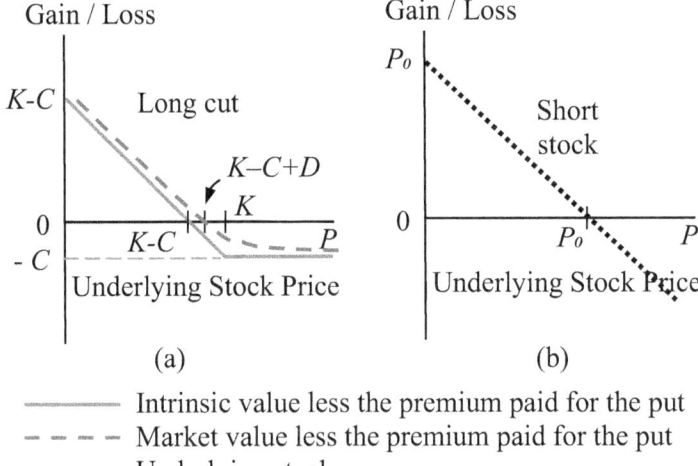

——— Intrinsic value less the premium paid for the put
– – – – Market value less the premium paid for the put
·········· Underlying stock

Figure 10-4: The gain/loss diagrams for (a) a long put at expiration or exercise (the solid line) or if sold at the market value (the dashed curve) and (b) a short position of the underlying stock P; K is the put strike price, C is the premium paid for buying the put, D is the premium received for selling the put, P_0 is the underlying stock short sale price

10.3.3 Summary of Long Options vs Stock Positions

Let's discuss the advantages and disadvantages of the long options at expiration or exercise vs the matching underlying stock positions.

Suppose a long position of a certain stock is opened at market price P_0 and a long call position with the strike price K equal P_0 is opened by paying premium C for the call. The gain/loss diagrams for these two positions are shown in Figure 10-5(a). Both positions will gain if the price of the underlying stock goes up and lose if the price of the underlying stock drops.

In comparison of a call with the matching long stock position, the call protects the trader from the excessive loss if the underlying stock price drops below the call breakeven price (the strike price plus the premium paid for the call), limiting the maximum loss to the price paid for the stock. On the other hand, the long call position gains are by C less than the gains from the matching long stock position if the underlying stock price grows above the strike price.

Now, consider a short position of a stock opened at market price P_0 and a long put position of the same stock with the strike price K equal P_0 opened by paying premium C for the put. The gain/loss diagrams for these two positions are shown in Figure 10-5(b). The long put position protects the trader from the excessive losses if the underlying stock price rises above the stock purchased price. On the other hand, both, the short stock gains if the stock price falls below the stock short sale price ($K = P_0$) and the long put position is gaining if the stock price falls below the breakeven price which is by C lower than the strike orice. Note that the long put is gaining by C less than the short stock position because of the premium paid for the long put position.

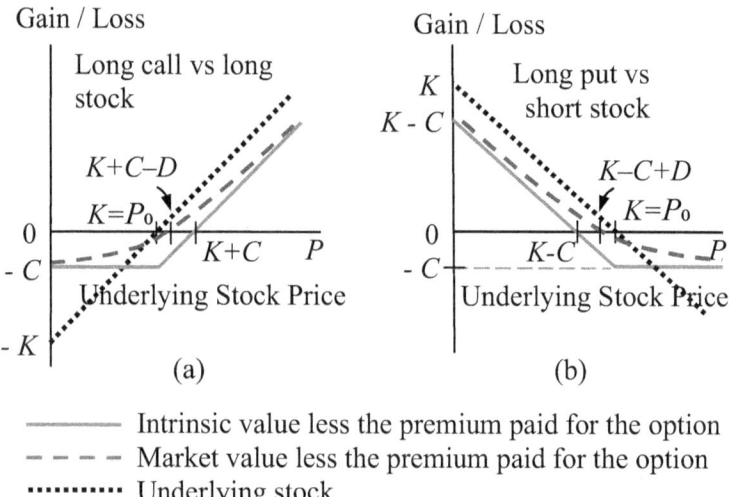

——— Intrinsic value less the premium paid for the option
– – – – Market value less the premium paid for the option
············ Underlying stock

Figure 10-5: The gain/loss diagrams for a long option at expiration or exercise (the solid line) or if sold at the market value (the dashed curve) vs the underlying stock position (the dotted line) (a) for a call and a long stock position and (b) for a put and the short stock position as a function of the underlying stock price P. K is the option strike price, C is the premium paid for the option, D is the premium received for selling the option, P_0 is the underlying stock price, at which the stock positions was opened

10.4 Short Options vs Stock Positions

By writing options (sell-to-open), the trader opens a short option position. It could be a short call or a short put position. In this section, we analyze a naked short option positions vs the matching positions of the underlying stock.

10.4.1 A Short Call vs a Short Stock Position

Let's compare a naked (short) call with the strike price K written at premium C with a short position of the underlying stock opened at the stock price P_0. The gain/loss diagram of the short call at expiration is shown in Figure 10-6(a) and the gain/loss diagram of the short position of the underlying stock is shown in Figure 10-6(b).

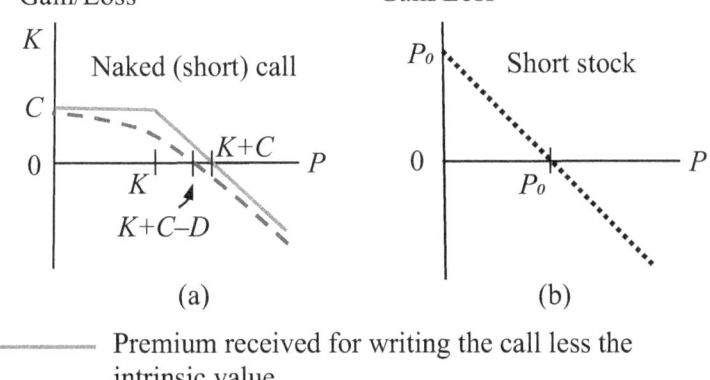

——— Premium received for writing the call less the intrinsic value
- - - - Premium received for writing the call less the market value paid the call to close the position
·········· Underlying stock

Figure 10-6: The gain/loss for (a) a naked (short) call at expiration or assignment and (b) a short position of the underlying stock as a function of the underlying stock price P, where K is the call strike price, C is the premium received from writing the call, D is the premium paid to buy the call to close the short call position, P_0 is the short stock sale price.

Both, the short call and the short underlying stock positions are targeting the underlying stock price downturn trend. The maximum possible gain with a short stock position is limited to the stock short sale price P_0, in case if the stock price drops to zero as shown in Figure 10-6(b). The maximum gain with the short call position is limited to the premium C received for writing the call (Figure 10-6(a)).

However, if the underlying stock price rises above the short sale price P_0, the stock short position turns into a loss with the unlimited possible loss, if the stock price keeps going up as shown in Figure 10-6(b). The possible loss with the short call position is also unlimited (Figure 10-6(a)). Thus, the naked (short) call position offers a gain limited to the premium C received writing the short call and unlimited potential loss. However, the naked call stays profitable with a cushion even if the underlying stock price rises above the strike price by the premium C received for writing the call.

10.4.2 A Short Put vs a Long Stock Position

Let's compare now a naked (short) put with the strike price K written at premium C with a long position of the underlying stock opened at the stock price P_0.

The gain/loss diagram of the short put at expiration is shown in Figure 10-7(a) and the gain/loss diagram of the long position of the underlying stock is shown in Figure 10-7(b).

Both, the short put position and the long underlying stock position are targeting the expected uptrend of the underlying stock price. both positions are gaining, if the underlying stock price keeps growing as shown in Figure 10-7(a). The maximum gain with the long stock position is unlimited while the maximum gain with the short put is limited to the premium C received when writing the put.

However, if the stock price drops below the stock purchase price P_0, the long stock position turns into a loss, with the maximum possible loss limited to the stock purchase price P_0 if the stock price drops to zero as shown in Figure 10-7(b). On the other hand, the maximum possible loss with the short put position is limited to the put's strike price less the premium received for the put (Figure 10-7(a)). Thus, the short put position offers some protection from the possible loss but limits a possible maximum gain. However, the naked put stays profitable with a cushion even the underlying stock price falls below the strike price by the premium C received for writing the put.

10 Trading Strategies with Single Options   101

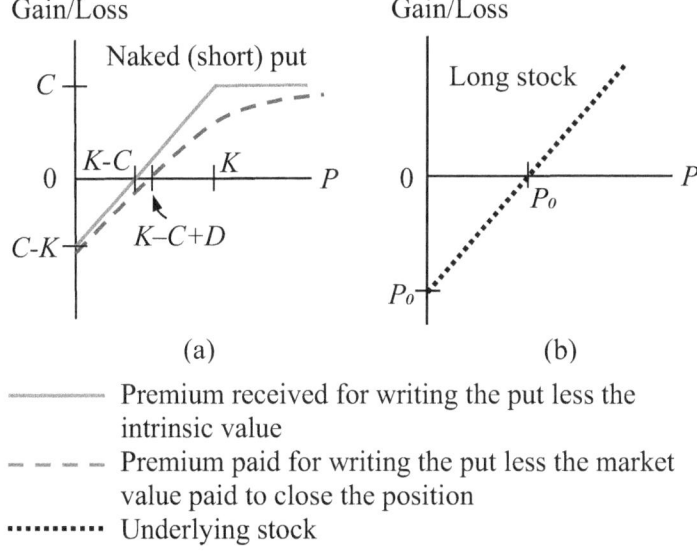

———— Premium received for writing the put less the intrinsic value
– – – – Premium paid for writing the put less the market value paid to close the position
·········· Underlying stock

Figure 10-7: The gain/loss for (a) a naked (short) put at expiration or assignment and (b) a long position of the underlying stock as a function of the underlying stock price P, where K is the call strike price, C is the premium received from writing the put, D is the premium paid to buy the put to close the short put position P_0 is the long stock purchase price.

10.4.3 Summary of Short Options vs Stock Positions

Let's compare a short position of a certain stock opened at market price P_0 with a short call position with the strike price $K = P_0$ written for premium C. The gain/loss diagrams for these two positions are shown in Figure 10-8(a). Both positions will gain if the price of the underlying stock declines and lose if the price of the underlying stock goes up.

In comparison of a short call with a matching short stock position, the short call provides a limited maximum gain equal the premium received for writing the call, if the call expires out-of-the-money. The gain for the short stock position can be higher if the stock price drops below $P_0 - C$. The short position is more profitable than the naked call if the stock price significantly drops. On the other hand, if the stock price increase, both positions start losing, but the short call loses by C less than the short stock position. The short call position stays profitable, if the stock underlying price does not change or changes within C form P_0.

Thus, the short stock position has the higher expectation of the gain than for the loss, if the stock price has the higher probability to drop than to rise. The naked call provides the limited return but gains even if the underlying stock price drops or even grows by C form P_0.

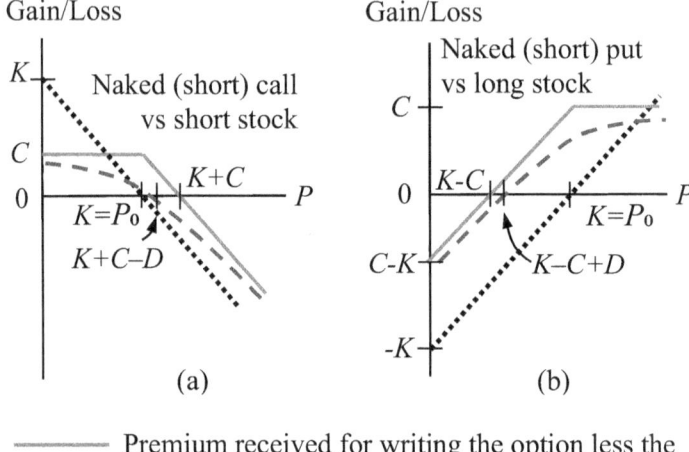

———— Premium received for writing the option less the intrinsic value
– – – – Premium received for writing the option less the market value
·········· Underlying stock

Figure 10-8: The gain/loss diagrams for (a) a naked call at expiration or assignment (the solid line) and if closed by buying at the market value (the dashed curve) vs a short position of the underlying stock (the dotted line) and (b) a naked put at expiration or assignment (the solid line) and if closed by buying at the market value (the dashed curve) vs a long position of the underlying stock (the dotted line) as a function of the underlying stock price P. K is the option strike price, C is the premium received for writing the option, D is the premium paid for buying the option to close its short position, P_0 is the underlying stock price, when the stock positions were opened

10 Trading Strategies with Single Options

Let's compare now a naked short call position with a short position of the underlying stock. Suppose a short position of a certain stock is opened at market price P_0 and a short call position was written at-the-money, i.e. with the strike price K ($K=P_0$), and the call writer received premium C for writing the call. The gain/loss diagrams for these two positions are shown in Figure 10-8(a). Both positions will gain, if the price of the underlying stock falls and lose is the price of the underlying stock goes up.

The short call position can be closed either by buying the call (the dashed curve in Figure 10-8(a)) or by the expiration or assignment (the solid line in Figure 10-8(a)). If the short call position is closed by buying the call, the gain/loss equals the difference between the premium received for writing the call and the premium paid for buying the call later to close the position. If the short call position expires or the call holder wants to exercise it, then the gain/loss from the naked short call position equals the premium received for writing the call less the intrinsic value of the call at the expiration or at the assignment.

Thus, if the call expires out-of-the-money, the call writer just keeps the premium at which he wrote the call. If the short call expires in-the-money or the call holder decides to exercise it before the expiration, the call writer gets the assignment. However, it the underlying stock price grows above the strike price but stays below the breakeven price, $K+C$, the call writer is still in gain from the transaction. On the other hand, if the stock price falls below the initial stock short sale price, $P_0=K$, the short stock position gains, but if stock price grows above the initial stock short sale price, $P_0=K$, the short stock position losses the money.

In comparison of a short call with a underlying short stock position, the short call provides a limited maximum gain equal the premium received for writing the call, if the call expires out-of-the-money. In contrast to the short call, the gain from the short stock position is limited to the initial stock price at which the short stock position was open, if the stock price falls to zero. Both, a short call and the short stock position have unlimited possible loss if the stock price grows. Then why to use a short call? The main reason for writing a call instead of opening a short stock position of the underlying stock is that the short call gains when the stock price stays unchanged or even slightly increases as clearly seen in Figure 10-8(a).

Thus, the gain/loss of the short stock position directly depends on the grows or decline of the stock price versus the initial price P_0. The naked call provides the lower maximum gain but stays profitable even if the underlying stock price stays unchanged or even slightly increases.

Let's compare now a short put position with a long position of the underlying stock. Suppose a long position of a certain stock is opened at market price P_0 and a short put position was open at-the-money, i.e. with the strike price K ($K=P_0$), and the put writer received premium C for writing the put. The gain/loss diagrams for these two positions are shown in Figure 10-8(b). Both positions will gain, if the price of the underlying stock goes up and lose is the price of the underlying stock declines.

The short put position can be closed either by buying the put (the dashed curve in Figure 10-8(b)) or by the expiration or assignment (the solid line in Figure 10-8(b)). If the short put position is closed by buying the put, the gain/loss equals the difference between the premium received for writing the put and the premium paid for buying the put later to close the position. If the short put position expires or the call holder decides to exercise it, then the gain/loss from the naked short put position equals the premium received for writing the call less the intrinsic value of the put at the expiration or at the assignment.

Thus if the put expires out-of-the-money, the put writer just keeps the premium at which he wrote the put. If the short put expires in-the-money or the put holder decides to exercise it before the expiration, the put writer gets the assignment. However, it the underlying stock price falls below the strike price but stays above the breakeven price, $K-C$, the put writer is still in gain from the transaction. On the other hand, if the stock price grows above the initial stock purchase price, $P_0=K$, the long stock position gains, but if stock price falls below the initial stock purchase price, $P_0=K$, the short stock position losses the money.

In comparison of a short put with a underlying long stock position, the short put provides a limited maximum gain equal the premium received for writing the put, if the put expires out-of-the-money. In contrast to the short put, the gain from the long stock position can is unlimited, if the stock price keeps going up. Then why to use a short put? The main reason for writing a put instead of opening a long stock position of the underlying stock is that the short put gains when the stock price stays unchanged or even slightly declines as clearly seen in Figure 10-8(b).

Thus, the gain/loss of the long stock position directly depends on the grows or decline of the stock price versus the initial price P_0.

10 Trading Strategies with Single Options

The naked put provides the limited return vs the long position of the underlying stock but gains even if the underlying stock price stays unchanged or even slightly drops.

10.5 Summary of Naked Calls and Puts

As it follows from the analysis above, naked options, i.e. naked calls (short calls) and naked puts (short puts), provide a viable profit generation mechanism for investors, if the investors have correctly predicted the underlying stock price trend and provide a protective price cushion in the amount received from selling the option short (sell-to-open). The rationale for naked (short) options is, mostly, that the time value of options declines with time left till expiration and becomes zero at the expiration. This provides the better cushion for the gain than the uncertainty with the underlying stock's price direction if open a long or short stock position. It means that naked options may work even when the stock price direction was wrongly predicted, but still stayed profitable within the price cushion that made it profitable.

For a better illustration of the sense of naked options, either naked calls or puts, assume that the option was written at-the-money, i.e. $K = P_0$ at the time of selling short where K is the option strike price and P_0 is the underlying stock price at the moment of short sale (sell-to-open). Assume also that, for some reasons, the option was at-the-money at the expiration date too, i.e. $P = K$ at the expiration. Under these conditions, the premium C, received from selling the option short (writing the option), was equal to the time value of the option due to the zero intrinsic value at that time. At the expiration, the option time value declines to zero. As a result, the naked option ends up with a gain equal to the option's initial time value V_{Time}^0. The profit from the naked option in this case (either call or put) was related to the time decay of the extrinsic (time) value of the option, rather than to the changes in the underlying stock prices. This is the essence of naked calls and puts.

Naked calls are profitable if the underlying stock price stays below $K+C$ at the assignment or expiration, but if the stock price rises above $K+C$, the naked call loses money and the loss is virtually unlimited if the stock price keeps going up, as shown in Figure 10-6(a) and Figure 10-8(a). Similarly, naked puts are profitable if the underlying stock price stays above $K-C$ at the assignment or expiration, but becomes a loss if the stock price falls below $K-C$.

However, the loss with a naked put is limited to $C-K$ if the stock price falls to zero as shown in Figure 7-1(a) and Figure 10-8(b).

It is also important to remember that naked options provide a price cushion in the range of C, i.e. naked calls are still profitable if the price of the underlying stock rises up to $K+C$ at the assignment or expiration and naked puts end up profitable if the stock price stays above $K-C$.

Naked options refer to the options strategy, when investors write (sell short) calls or puts to without hedging them with the long positions of the underlying security for calls or short positions of the underlying security for puts. Naked calls are sometimes referred to as "uncovered calls" or "short calls" and naked puts as "uncovered puts" or "short puts."

Naked options present an aggressive and lucrative strategy, but are associated with high risk, particularly with naked calls due to unlimited potential losses associated with them.

- The *maximum gain* from a naked call or put is limited to the amount received from selling them short.
- A *naked call ends up with a loss* if the underlying stock price grows above the call strike price plus the premium received from selling the call.
- The *maximum loss from a naked call* is unlimited if the underlying stock price continues to grow.
- A *naked put ends up with a loss* if the underlying stock price declines below the put strike price less the premium received from selling the put.
- The *maximum loss from a naked put* is limited to the premium for selling the put less the strike price if the underlying stock price falls to zero.

Self-Testing Questions and Exercises

Questions

1. What is the relationship between a short call and a matching long call?
2. What is the relationship between a short put and a matching long put?

10 Trading Strategies with Single Options

3. What is the difference between a naked call and a long put?
4. What is the difference between a naked put and a long call?
5. What is the difference between a long call and a long stock?
6. What is the difference between a short call and a short stock?
7. What is the difference between a long put and a short stock?
8. What is the difference between a short put and a long stock?
9. What is the rationale for naked calls and naked puts?
10. How would a naked option, call or put, expire (with profit or with loss) if the price of the underlying stock at the expiration equals the price of the stock at the time of writing the option initiation?
11. What is the highest potential gain/loss for a naked call?
12. What is the highest potential gain/loss for a naked put?
13. What is a breakeven price of the underlying security of an option?
14. What is a breakeven range for the underlying security of an option?
15. What is the difference between closing a long option, call or put, position by selling it or by exercising it?
16. What is the difference between closing a short option position, call or put, by buying the matching option in the market it or by expiration OTM or assignment ITM?

Exercises

In the following exercises, please ignore price spread (ask minus bid) and transaction commissions, unless some special condition is specified in the exercise.

1. A call with the strike price $41.00 was purchased at-the-money for $3.20 and sold in one week for $2.10, when the underlying stock price was $42.00. What was the time value of the call, when the call was sold?
2. A long put position was opened at-the-money with premium of $4.10, when the underlying stock price was $47.00 and closed in one week for $2.80, when the underlying stock price was $48.00. What was the time value of the put, when the put position was closed?
3. A call with the strike price of $42.00 was written at $7.00 per call when the underlying stock was traded at $45.00 per share.

What was the time value of the call at that time?

4. A call with the strike price of $50.00 was written for $4.00 when the underlying stock's price was $48.00 per share. Draw the gain/loss chart for the naked call at expiration.

5. Stock ABA is currently traded at the spot price of $38.00 and a put with the strike price of $38.00 was sold short at $3.00. Draw the gain/loss chart for the naked put at expiration.

6. A put with the strike price of $40.00 was written at $6.20 when the price of the underlying stock was $38.00 per share. Draw the gain/loss chart for the naked put.

7. One contract of calls with the strike price $90.00 was written at $8.00 at the time when the underlying stock was traded at $89.00. Another trader opened a short position of that underlying stock at $89.00. The stock, at the call expiration, was traded for $95.00. What is the gain or loss from this call at the expiration and from the short stock position at the same time?

8. A put with the strike price $52.00 was sold short at $12.50 at the time when the underlying stock was traded at $45.00. Another trader opened a long stock position of that underlying stock at $45.00. What is the gain or loss from this put at the expiration and from the long stock position at the same time?

11 Trend Strategies

11.1 Choosing the Strategy for the Expected Trend

Investment in the stock market is always associated with risk. Knowledgeable and experienced investors are capable to choose the best matching strategy to maximize their gains and minimizing risk. Though there is no silver bullet in the stock market to guarantee you success, a thoughtful choice of the best matching strategies may help in this endeavor. The choice of strategies includes the most optimal portfolio management best fitting your investment goals, the best usage of technical, fundamental, and sentimental indicators to find the best time for opening and closing the investment positions, many other strategic approaches, and finally, the choice between long and short stock and option positions. In this book and in this chapter, we will discuss the choice of long and short stocks versus single long and short option positions for a single stock.

11.2 Long Stock, Long Call, and Short Put

If the investor expects the stock price uptrend, then the most natural choice is to open a long stock position of that stock. However, the actual stock price trend may go in the wrong direction of the expected trend causing a loss with the long stock position. Using options may help hedging the potential losses.

Figure 11-1 shows the gain/loss diagram for a long stock position (the solid line), a long call position at the expiration or exercise (dashed line), and for short put at the expiration or assignment (dotted line). Both option positions were open ATM (at-the-money). It means that the strike prices for the options were equal the stock price at the time, when the option positions were open, i.e. $K=P_0$.

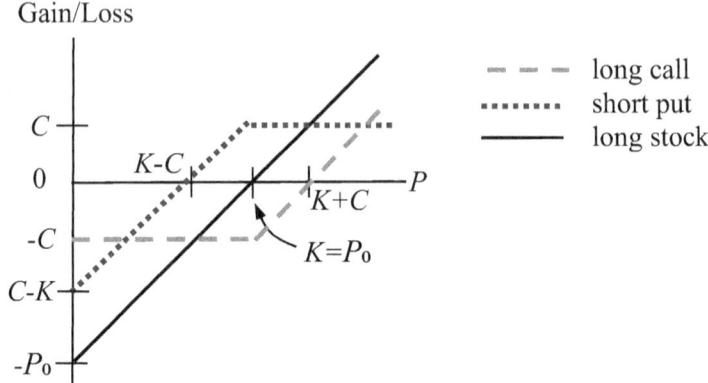

Figure 11-1: The gain/loss diagram for a long stock position (solid line ———), a long call position at the expiration or exercise (dashed line – – –), and for short put at the expiration or assignment (dotted line ·········). Both option positions were open at-the-money

As is evident from Figure 11-1, a long call and a short put work for the uptrend of the stock price, in the same direction as a long stock position. However, there are the following differences between these three strategies:

- The long stock position shows a linear gain for prices above P_0 and a linear loss for prices below P_0.
- The long call shows linear gain for prices above P_0+C, a constant loss of the premium paid for the call, C, for prices below P_0 and a linear loss from C to zero for the cushion price range between P_0 and P_0+C (the same as $K+C$ in this case)
- The short put shows a constant gain equal the premium C received for writing the put for prices above P_0, a linear loss for prices below P_0-C, and a linear gain in the cushion range between P_0-C (the same as $K-C$ in this case) and P_0.

Choosing a long call (a dashed line in Figure 11-1) instead of a long stock (a solid line in Figure 11-1) position, the investor expects the stock price growth, but wants to limit a possible loss by amount C, the premium paid for the call, if the stock price falls, and for this, agrees to reduce the possible gain by the same amount C versus the long stock position, if the stock price goes in the right direction, i.e. goes up.

On the other hand, choosing a short put (a dotted line in Figure 11-1) instead of a long stock position (a solid line in Figure 11-1), the investor also expects the stock price to grow, but agrees to limit a possible gain to amount C, the premium received for writing the put, if the stock price rises, but for this, extends the gain range of the stock price by the cushion C to P_0-C and reduce the loss by amount C versus the long stock position, if the stock price goes in the wrong direction, i.e. falls.

Thus, all three variants—a long stock position, a long call and a short put—can be used, if the investor expects the stock price uptrend. However, each of these three variants has its own pros and cons as of the possible gain, loss, and risk.

11.3 Short Stock, Short Call, and Long Put

Figure 11-2 shows the gain/loss diagram for a short stock position (solid line), a short call position at the expiration or assignment (dashed line), and for long call at the expiration or exercise (dotted line). Both option positions were open ATM (at-the-money). It means that the strike prices for the options were equal the stock price at the time, when the option positions were open.

Choosing a long put (a dotted line in Figure 11-1) instead of a short stock (a solid line in Figure 11-2) position, the investor expects the stock price to fall, but wants to limit a possible loss by amount C, the premium paid for the put, if the stock price increases, and for this, agrees to reduce the possible gain by the same amount C versus the short stock position, if the stock price falls as expected.

On the other hand, choosing a short call (a dashed line in Figure 11-2) instead of a short stock position (a solid line in Figure 11-2), the investor also expects the stock price to fall, but agrees to limit a possible gain to amount C, the premium received for writing the put, if the stock price falls as expected, but for this, extends the gain range of the stock price by the cushion C to P_0+C and reduce the loss by amount C versus the short stock position, if the stock price goes in the wrong direction, i.e. goes up.

Thus, all three variants—a short stock position, a long put and a short call—can be used, if the investor expects the stock price to fall However, each of these three variants has its own pros and cons as of the possible gain, loss, and risk.

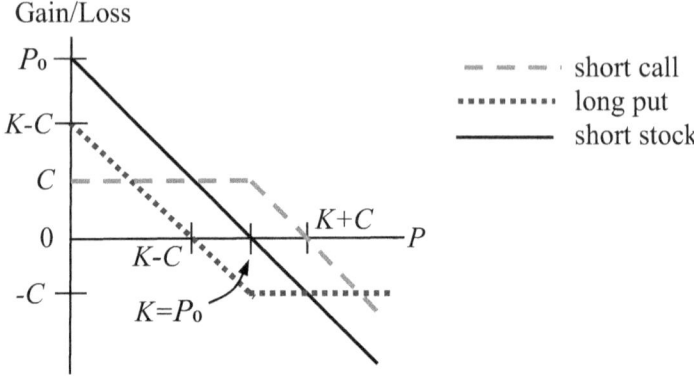

Figure 11-2: The gain/loss diagram for a short stock position (solid line ———), a short call position at the expiration or assignment (dashed line — — —), and for long call at the expiration or exercise (dotted line ·········). Both option positions were open at-the-money

11.4 Summary of Single Options

Long and short options and stock positions offer a variety of investment opportunities targeting different price trend expectations.

Long and short stock positions have "linear" gain/loss dependency on the stock price, which could be equally gaining or losing depends on the direction of the stock price trend.

Long options, calls and puts, offer some protection, if the underlying stock price goes in the unexpected direction, by limiting the loss to the amount (premium) paid for the option. This protection comes with the reduction of the possible gain versus the matching underlying stock position, by the same amount of the premium paid for the option, if the underlying stock goes in the expected direction.

Sort options, calls and puts, are originated by writing the options. Single short options, also referred to as naked options, offer limited gains equal the amount (premium) received for writing the options, if the underlying stock price trends to the expected direction, up or down, or even stays unchanged. On the other hand, if the underlying stock price goes in the wrong direction, the short options offer some price cushion relative to the matching underlying stock position. The major advantage short options is that they stay profitable if the underlying stock price stays unchanged and even slightly goes to the wrong direction.

As we have discussed in this book, single options, long and short, offer interesting investment opportunities. More complex opportunities come with the combination of options with stocks and options, such as covered and protective calls and puts, straddles, strangles, spreads butterflies, condors and other. A variety of such combinations including their usage, opportunities, as well as their pros and cons will be discussed in the separate book.

Self-Testing Questions and Exercises

Questions

1. What is the difference between a long stock, a long ATM call, and a short ATM put?
2. What is the difference between a short stock, a short ATM call, and a long ATM put?
3. What stock price trend is advantageous for a long stock, a long ATM call, and a short ATM put?
4. What stock price trend is advantageous for a short stock, a short ATM call, and a long ATM put?
5. What is the difference between writing an option and selling the option short?

Index

activation conditions, 31
all or none, 31
American option, 52
American options, 6, 52, 53
annual volume, 34
ask, 26
assignment (options), 52, 53, 62, 63, 64, 67, 68, 69, 70, 72, 73, 74, 80, 84, 105
ATM, 15
at-the money, 68
at-the-money, 16, 68, 72, 79, 105
at-the-money (ATM), 15
automatic option exercise and assignment, 33
bid, 26
binomial model (options), 43
Black-Sholes model, 43
breakeven price, 69, 71, 73, 74, 80, 82, 83, 84
breakeven range, 70, 71, 72, 73, 74, 76, 77, 81, 82, 83, 84, 85
buy- to-close, 31
buy-to-close, 29, 30, 38, 62
buy-to-open, 29, 31
call, 5, 7, 11, 12, 14, 15, 18, 26, 31
call assignment, 32
call seller, 32
call short, 68
CBOE, 10
CBOE Holding Inc., 10
Chicago Board of Trade, 10
Chicago Board Options Exchange (CBOE), 10
CME Group, 25
contract (options), 61
contracts (options), 25, 27, 31, 35
cost of carry, 47, 48
daily volume, 34
day order, 31
delta (δ), 44
derivatives, 7, 25
European options, 6
exchange-traded options, 10, 27
execution price, 31
exercise, 15
exercise (options), 6, 38, 53, 55, 56, 57, 62, 68
exercise option), 12
expiration, 5, 6, 12, 20, 31
expiration (options), 62, 63, 64, 67, 68, 69, 71, 72, 73, 74, 75, 80, 84, 105
expiration date, 11, 12, 20, 26
expiring in-the-money options, 33
extrinsic value, 13, 17, 20, 23, 43, 65
fill or kill, 31
futures, 7
gain/loss for a naked call, 70
gamma (γ), 45
Greeks (options), 43, 48
GTC, 31
hedging, 106
high return strategies, 51
high risk, 106
historical volatility, 43
hundred options per each contract, 61
implied volatility, 44
initial public offering, 10, 28
instances of listed options, 29
in-the-money, 15, 32, 33, 68, 69, 71, 74, 79
in-the-money (ITM), 14, 15
intrinsic value, 13, 14, 15, 16, 17, 23, 32, 33, 43, 54, 55, 56, 57, 62, 64, 67, 68, 69, 71, 79, 80, 82, 105
IPO, 28
ITM, 14, 15
leverage investment, 49
leverage trading strategy, 41
limit, 31
listed call options, 11
listed options, 9, 10, 25, 28, 29, 52
listed standardized options, 10
long call, 53, 54, 57
long options, 53, 58

Index

long position, 15
long put, 53, 58
market, 31
maximum gain, 72, 83, 106
maximum loss, 106
maximum possible gain, 69, 71, 72, 74, 76, 77, 79, 81, 84, 85
maximum possible loss, 57, 58
maximum possible profit, 83
maximum potential loss, 79
monthly volume, 34
naked (short) call, 70, 72
naked (short) options, 105
naked call, 62, 64, 67, 68, 69, 70, 71, 72, 73, 74, 75, 76, 77, 79, 84, 105, 106
naked calls, 76, 106
naked option, 70, 73, 74, 84, 105
naked options, 64, 106
naked put, 62, 64, 79, 80, 81, 82, 83, 84, 85, 105, 106
naked puts, 106
non-negotiable, 28
number of contracts (options), 31
OCC, 10, 28
OCC randomly assigns in-the-money options, 34
OCC rule, 33
open a short option position, 61
open interest, 29, 34, 35, 36, 38
option, 5, 7, 8, 12, 15, 16
option assignment, 32, 52, 53, 64, 67, 68, 69, 70, 72, 73, 74, 80, 84, 105
option buyer (holder), 51
Option Clearing Corporation (OCC), 10
option contact, 62
option exercise, 6, 32, 38, 53, 55, 56, 57, 68
option expiration, 6, 31, 64, 67, 71, 72, 73, 74, 75, 80, 84, 105
option expiration, 68
option expiration, 69
option Greeks, 48
option holder, 6, 32
option order, 32
option premium, 16
option quotation, 25

option seller, 6, 32, 51
option short sale, 82
option to buy, 12
option to sell, 12
option type, 11, 26, 31
options, 7, 8, 11, 15, 16, 19, 25
Options Clearing Corporation, 10
options Greeks, 43, 48
options listed on stock exchanges, 9
order action, 31
order routing, 31
order timing, 31
OTM, 15, 16
out-of-the-money, 15, 68, 72, 79, 80
out-of-the-money (OTM), 15, 16
potential gain, 57, 58
premium, 7, 8, 17, 23, 51
premium (options), 54, 69, 105, 106
price cushion, 72, 73, 76, 83, 84, 85, 105, 106
price of the underlying stock, 71, 72, 73, 74, 79
price range cushion, 85
protective strategies, 51
put, 5, 8, 11, 12, 14, 15, 18, 26, 31
put assignment, 32
quotation (options), 25
rho (ρ), 47
risk, 85
risk-free interest, 48
risk-free interest rates, 44
secondary public offering, 28
sell option short, 62, 63, 64
sell options short, 61
sell short (options), 62, 72, 74, 80
sell short calls, 106
sell short puts, 106
sell the option short, 105
sell the put short, 79, 80
selling options short, 28
selling shares short, 28
selling short a call, 68
selling short an option contract, 28
selling the put short, 80

sell-to-close, 29, 30, 31, 63
sell-to-open, 29, 30, 31, 34, 38, 61, 62, 63, 68, 69, 71, 72, 74, 76, 77, 80, 85, 105
short call, 61, 64, 67, 69, 71, 105
short call position, 61
short calls, 106
short options, 61, 65
short position, 8, 15, 29, 55
short put, 61, 64, 79, 105
short puts, 106
short sale (options), 71, 74, 80, 105
special instructions, 31
SPO, 28
spot price, 7, 8, 13, 14, 15, 16, 17, 18, 19, 52, 69, 83
spot stock price, 14
standard deviation, 43
standardized options, 9, 10
stock price, 74, 77
stock price cushion, 82
stock spot price, 16, 17, 18, 19
stop, 31
strike price, 5, 6, 7, 11, 12, 14, 15, 16, 17, 18, 19, 26, 31, 32, 44, 51, 52, 57, 63, 68, 69, 71, 73, 75, 76, 77, 81, 82, 83, 84, 85, 90, 92, 95, 97, 98, 99, 101, 102, 106
strike prices, 17
swaps, 7
theta (θ), 46
ticker symbol, 11, 26
time left till expiration, 23
time until expiration, 44

time value, 13, 17, 18, 19, 20, 21, 22, 23, 52, 54, 55, 64, 65, 69, 71, 73, 79, 81, 82, 84, 85, 105
time value decay, 20, 21, 22
total value of an option, 14
trading action, 31
trading instruments, 7
trading volume, 34, 35, 36
trailing stop, 31
uncovered calls, 106
uncovered puts, 106
underlying price, 44
underlying security, 11, 68
underlying stock, 6, 7, 12, 13, 14, 15, 16, 17, 19, 21, 26, 31, 32, 33, 51, 55, 57, 69, 72, 73, 74, 76, 82, 83, 84, 85
underlying stock price, 14, 17, 18, 19, 57, 67, 68, 69, 72, 75, 79, 81, 97, 98, 102, 105, 106
underlying stock spot price, 17, 18, 19
unlisted options, 10, 12
volatility, 43
volume, 34, 35, 36, 38
write (term), 28
write a call, 62
write a put, 62
write an option, 61
write an option contract, 28
writing a call, 51, 68
writing a put, 51
writing an options, 28
writing the call, 72, 76, 77
writing the option, 63
writing the put, 85

www.ingramcontent.com/pod-product-compliance
Lightning Source LLC
Chambersburg PA
CBHW071416210526
45465CB00001B/413